TYPOLOGY

TYPE DESIGN FROM

THE VICTORIAN ERA

TO THE DIGITAL AGE

STEVEN HELLER

AND LOUISE FILI

CHRONICLE BOOKS

SAN FRANCISCO

ACKNOWLEDGMENTS

The authors are indebted to Mary Jane Callister for her splendid design and her devotion to this project. Thanks also to Alan Rapp, editor at Chronicle Books, for his enthusiasm and expert shepherding of this book through all its stages; and to Mark Batlle, for assisting during the research stage. Further gratitude goes to Lesley Hathaway, at Louise Fili Ltd, for production assistance; Bill LeBlond, senior editor; Michael Carabetta, art director; Patricia Evangelista, designer, at Chronicle Books for their continued support. And a tip of the hat to our agent, Sarah Jane Freymann.

Compiling the material for a book of this scope required considerable aid from many individuals and institutions. We are most grateful to the following: James Fraser, Fairleigh Dickinson University Library; Elaine Lustig Cohen, Ex Libris; Ric Grefe, the American Institute of Graphic Arts; Carol Wahler, the Type Directors Club; Bride Whalen, the Society of Publication Designers; John Berry, the International Typeface Corporation; Rudy VanderLans, Emigre; Art Spiegelman, Raw Books and Graphics; Roger Black, Roger Black Associates; Irving Oaklander, Oaklander Books; Kathy Leff, Wolfsonian Institution; Franc Nunoo-Quarcoo, the University of Maryland; Betsy Kopshina, GarageFonts; Bob Aufuldish, FontBoy; Jonathan Hoefler, Hoefler Type Foundry; Neville Brody, FUSE and Research Studio; Tobias Frere-Jones, Font Bureau; Seymour Chwast, Push Pin Studio; Milton Glaser and Marla Garfield, Milton Glaser Inc.; Ed Benguiat; Naum Kashdan; Chet Helms, Atelier Dore; Victor Moscoso; Laurie Burns; April Greiman; Katherine McCoy; Jeffery Keedy; Jonathan Barnbrook; Rick Poynor; Peter Girardi, Funny Garbage; Julie Belcher and Kevin Bradley, Yee-Haw Studios; Daniel Pelavin; Ed Fella; Josh Berger, Plazm Fonts; Paula Scher, Pentagram; Marion Rand; Ivan Chermayeff, Chermayeff & Geismar; Wolfgang Weingart; Rudolph de Harak; Martin Solomon; Mirko Ilić; Jeff Roth; Simon Rendell; Alex Steinweiss; Bart Crosby; Michael Worthington; Tibor Kalman and Marta Weiss, M&Co; Museum für Gestaltung Zürich; Staatliche Museen Preußischer Kulturbesitz, Berlin; Museum of Modern Art, New York; Galerie Pabst, Vienna; Erik Spiekermann; David Batterham, David Batterham Books; Robert and Dorothy Emerson, R&D Emerson Books; George Theofiles, Miscellaneous Man; Charles Spencer Anderson, CSA Archive; John Plunkett, Wired; and the Walker Art Center.

Book design by Mary Jane Callister / Louise Fili Ltd.

www.chroniclebooks.com

THE AMERICAN PRINTER

for MAY

VOLUME NUMBER NINETY-EIGHT / ISSUE NUMBER FIVE

Price 25 Cents a Copy

$3.00 a Year

I N T R O D U C T I O N

"THE BUSINESS OF PRINTED LETTERING HAS NOW, UNDER THE SPUR OF
COMMERCIAL COMPETITION, GOT ALTOGETHER OUT AND HAND AND GONE MAD."

—ERIC GILL, *AN ESSAY ON TYPOGRAPHY*, 1930

Type means many things to many people. For the designer, it is an art. For the compositor, it is a craft. For the typehouse proprietor, it is a business. And for the reader, it is what typographer Beatrice Warde called "the voice of the page." Before addressing the focus of this book—the artistic goals and aesthetic concerns of type designers—it is useful to consider type from the standpoint of a business, indeed an industry. In this light, it is a fairly significant industry, with thousands of foundries and sup-

pliers, past and present, provid-
ing wood, hot-metal, film, and digital type to all kinds of media.
In addition to the sincere efforts put forth into improving mass
communication through more efficient type design, it was business concerns, not solely artistic impulse, that accelerated the state
that Eric Gill referred to in his time, and this continues today.
Even if one does not subscribe to his notion of "madness," fervent
marketplace competition has contributed to the spawning of many more faces than will ever be used effectively. Dating back to the nascence of commercial type manufacture in America and Europe in the mid-nineteenth century, critics in the printing trade journals asserted that an over-abundance of wood and metal type styles, including degraded variations or reinterpretations of original designs, littered the market. While attacking the seemingly insatiable need for perpetual novelty, these critics proposed standards to control those degradations that had become popular among the commercial printers who produced the lion's share of printed material. In one of his more vitriolic attacks, the American type master Frederic Goudy spoke for many of his peers in a 1912 article titled "The Art in Type Design" he wrote for *The Monotype Recorder:* "The meaningless lines or excrescences upon which so many modern designers, without ability to reach

OPPOSITE: THE AMERICAN PRINTER, *periodical cover, 1933. Designer unknown.*
ABOVE: WIRED, *periodical cover, 1997. Designer: John Plunkett.*

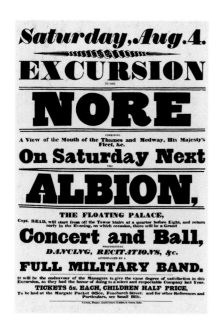

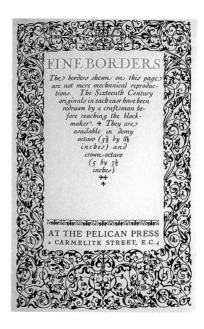

the higher beauties, rely, in their endeavor to conceal their lack of genius or taste, were never present in the type of the golden age of typography." The golden age of which he speaks is the sixteenth century, when some of the classic "humanist" faces (Bodoni, Garamond, Jensen) were introduced. Nevertheless, Goudy was one of the most prodigious of all the early-twentieth-century type designers.

Although Goudy's work adhered to strict self-imposed standards of art and craft, his rationale for producing so many designs was by no means entirely altruistic. He indeed created alphabets for the pure pleasure of exploring classic form and reviving historical precedents ("Those old guys stole our best ideas," he once said), but many of his faces were developed in a climate of soaring commercial competition among type foundries that demanded a consistent flow of new products. Goudy Stout, for example, a stubby bastardization (or derivation) of Ultra Bodoni with letters that recall Charlie Chaplin's vagabond gait, was admittedly produced to fulfill the need that typehouses had for a viable novelty advertising face. That business issues motivated the vast majority of type design is by no means a revelation, but given recent examinations in print and exhibitions of type as a popular art form, it is important to put the motivations into perspective.

Type—especially headline or display type—is not impervious to fashions and trends; rather, it is influenced by them. As the means by which the written word is communicated, a type's form

LEFT: EXCURSION, *advertisement, c. 1865. Designer unknown.* CENTER: SCHRIFTEN ATLAS, *title page, 1898. Designer unknown.* RIGHT: FINE BORDERS, *advertisement, c. 1895. Designer unknown.*

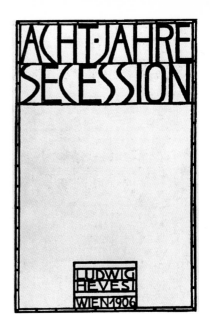

is often dictated by various factors occurring during the time of its conception. While certain typefaces are created to be universal, others are made purposefully to elicit a specific ephemeral aesthetic. Art Nouveau types of the late nineteenth century employed the sinuous and curvilinear shapes found in the furniture and fashion of that era, while, almost a century later, grunge type employs the brute scratches and scrawls evocative of contemporary style. Even some of the more neutral (or universal) faces, such as Helvetica and Univers, are indicative of a period in cultural, technological, and economic history, as well as a movement in design history. The archetypes of various designed objects, from cars to telephones, define their specific periods, just as original typefaces underscore moments and movements in time. Because of this, certain typefaces go in and out of currency at a speed commensurate with other cultural ephemera—sometimes even faster.

Whether working with hot-metal or digital fontography, foundries, which traditionally commission *and* manufacture type, have produced designs based on perceived commercial potential. Aesthetics may be a deciding factor in the overall conception of typology, but catering to the zeitgeist and to those who buy into it is just as important. Ever since the dawn of modern consumerism in the mid-nineteenth century and the advent of mass advertising to promote the influx of wares, type has been used to help promote and sell every kind of product. In the years when goods were hawked from the backs of wagons and the porches of general stores, typefaces on

LEFT: XXME EXPOSITION DU SALON DES CENT, *poster, 1896. Designer: Alphonse Mucha.* CENTER: AUGSBURG, *type specimen, c. 1905. Designer unknown.* RIGHT: ACHT JAHRE SECESSION, *catalog cover, 1906. Designer unknown.*

posters and handbills were designed to be as loud as the pitchmen who screamed at the passersby. Typefaces of this kind were not meant just to be read, but to be experienced. They were not simply vessels of meaning, but components of larger attractions intended to stir the awareness, if not the appetites, of the audience. Nevertheless, type was not a bit player in this drama. In the years before electronic mass media, type served as the means to differentiate products and ideas. In the nineteenth century, novelty fat-faces (the same types used for circus and theatrical posters) imbued products with a kind of fanfare—the typographic equivalent of loud banging drums and klieg lights. The reason that so many type styles currently exist is that the turn-of-the-century advertising boom required a large number of different styles in order to simulate diverse voices.

Thus in the first three decades of the twentieth century, type foundries were required to keep diverse stocks on hand because advertisers demanded constantly replenished stores of novelty faces. Designers were therefore routinely called upon to amplify old letterforms to give the appearance of the new. The result was that they often indiscriminately created slews of bastardized faces that eschewed classical typographic standards of grace and subtlety in favor of expediency. Nonetheless, in addition to *au courant* styles, old standbys were always in demand to fulfill the more traditional needs of readability and legibility.

Since not all text is equal in depth, breadth, or meaning, typefaces from the early twentieth

LEFT: BERNHARD ANTIQUA, *type specimen, c. 1910. Designer: Lucian Bernhard.* CENTER: JEDERMANN SEIN EIGNER FUSSBALL, *periodical cover, 1919. Designer: John Heartfield.* RIGHT: RICHARD DARTELMES, *theater program cover, 1927. Designer unknown.*

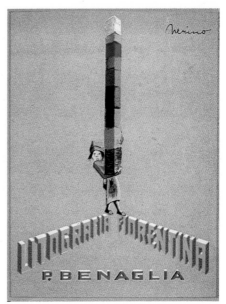

century were designed to be used in a variety of contexts. Like automobiles, some were engineered for pure utility, while others were more for sport. Some faces were better for lengthy, uninterrupted reading, while others were best for brief tracts and blurbs. Likewise, some faces were suited for young eyes; others were better for old. While display faces were, and continue to be, ephemeral, text faces, which must be more conservative by the nature of their function, have also been subjected to fashion. Although legibility has traditionally been the goal of type designers, some text faces have been designed to act more like wallpaper or background than the instrument for conveying meaning clearly. This is not just unique to the postmodern era's proliferation of quirky digital faces; throughout history designers have used type as "gray matter."

Three considerations have governed type design since the industry's beginning. Utility (how a face functions) and aesthetics (how it looks on a printed page) govern qualities of readability and legibility, while style affects what cultural code a typeface evokes. In the Victorian era, the changing concerns in type design, as Nicolette Gray describes in her 1938 book *Nineteenth Century Ornamented Types and Title Pages*, were not those of individual designers but a reflection of the tenor of their society. In fact, many of the most popular faces were designed by anonymous employees of commercial foundries; today some of these foundries are remembered, but the designers are largely forgotten. Style was not the offspring of a marriage of utility and aesthetics,

LEFT: DIE FORM, *periodical cover, 1926. Designer: Joost Schmidt.* CENTER: REMINGTON!, *advertisements, 1927. Designer: Bortnyik Sandor.* RIGHT: LITOGRAFIA FIORENTINA, *advertisement, 1932. Designer: Nerino.*

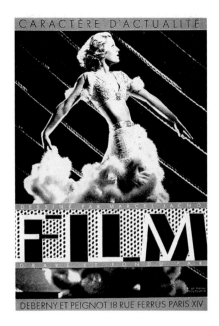

but rather an overlay imposed on the problem of designing a total alphabet. The aim of both foundries and printers was always to supply the public with novelties that attracted and pleased. "To succeed in this they had to keep in exact touch with the mood of the moment," wrote Gray. "Their businesses being purely commercial, considerations of scholarship, individual personality or typographical principle do not blur the contact. The result is a communal art as pure as that of any primitive society."

In the 1890s, most of the public did not understand the meaning of typographic quality. Only the cognoscenti—designers and printers—fretted about the state of the art, and a negative reaction to the primitive nature and crass commercialism that was rampant in the type business emerged among a growing number of the more sophisticated fine printers and applied artists. Their objections gave rise to a benchmark printing revival among designers in the United States and Europe who had an understanding of historical traditions. Ever since the sixteenth century, when the first capital letters were traced off Rome's Trajan Column, the monument on which appears the motherlode of roman type, serious type designers have pledged fealty to this Platonic letterform and have sought to make the perfect interpretations of original typographic form. When the respected English artist, author, and philosopher William Morris turned his attention to type design and printing and began producing work through his Kelmscott Press, historical

LEFT: FILM, *type specimen, 1934. Type designer: Marcel Janco.* CENTER: POWER, *theater poster, c. 1934. Designer unknown.* RIGHT: BOLD DISPLAY, *alphabet, c. 1939. Type designer unknown.*

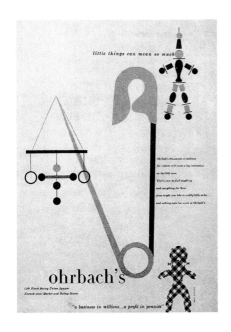

revivalism and preservationism hit the type business like a ton of hot metal.

The historicists, with Morris in the vanguard, reacted against the unrestrained typeplay of late-nineteenth-century Europe—what Nicolette Gray later described as an "insignificant contribution to the whole art" and typographer and historian Carl Purington Rollins, in a 1958 *Printing and Graphic Arts* article, called the "anemic type and presswork" of the 1880s. Gray reported that "the Victorians lost the idea of good type to read," implying that although display lettering of the era was intriguing, few developments advanced for text made a lasting impression. Morris changed that, and around the turn of the century, Americans Frederic Goudy, Will Bradley, D. B. Updike, and Bruce Rogers, among others, followed with various historical derivations that paid homage to, yet purportedly improved upon, the old designs. These revived types, which were originally used for books and periodicals that these men designed themselves, were eventually made available for wider consumption through the leading type businesses, notably American Type Founders, Inland Type Foundry, Barnhard and Spindler, Monotype, and Linotype. Goudy himself served as art director of the Monotype Company and saw to it that new types were developed for use on the Monotype machine that did not, as he put it, "sacrifice the ideals for which he stood."

The need to maintain high standards was not always at odds with making viable business decisions about what should be marketed. The history of type design is littered with types

LEFT: OHRBACH'S, *advertisement, c. 1945. Designer: Erik Nitsche.* CENTER: DIE GUTE FORM, *poster, 1954. Designer: Armin Hofmann.* RIGHT: MERLE MARSICANO, *poster, 1962. Designer: Rudolph de Harak.*

designed for the sake of expedience, and some of those were, and are, exemplary. Even Goudy, who was proprietor of his own press, did not oppose making novelty faces—"novelty keeps things fresh and alive," he wrote. Nevertheless, he felt that new things that were merely old things "newly advertised" were a pox on type design in general. When Goudy entered the type business in the late 1890s, he had to reconcile many of the issues that subsequently challenged type designers, such as how to design type that is fresh yet part of the continuum and how one designs for the masses and maintains artistic individuality.

One could argue that when tossed together into the great hellbox of history, all type tends to blend together. As long as the same basic alphabet is used, there are really few fundamental differences between type designs. Only stylistic variety is evident, but the history of type design is more amazing than that. While the same twenty-six letters are repeated, both the superficial qualities of the look and feel of a typeface, and the technical aspects such as weight and spacing are uniquely different in so many cases. Throughout the centuries since type design and manufacture became an industry, type has been a renewable and replenishable commodity. Although some critics assail the compulsion for ever more new faces, at the very least type, and by extension graphic design, benefits from not reverting into stagnation.

Typology: Type Design From the Victorian Era to the Digital Age is not a formal history of

LEFT: DREAM BOOK (PUSH PIN GRAPHIC), *periodical cover, 1966. Designer: Seymour Chwast.* CENTER: VANITY FAIR, *periodical cover (maquette) 1983. Designer: Henrietta Condak.* RIGHT: WORK SPIRIT, *periodical cover, 1988. Designer: April Greiman.*

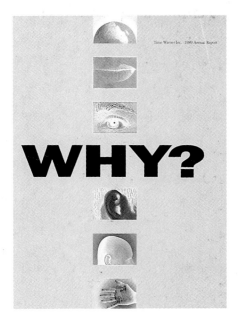

printing types, but rather a visual survey of the rich legacy left to us by type designers for over one hundred years. The purpose of this book is to examine commercial type design—with emphasis on headline or display types—from the pre-Modern to Postmodern eras. The thesis and organizing structure is that twentieth-century Modernism serves as the touchstone around which the past century of type design can be measured and compared. Therefore, type design can efficiently be categorized by its proximity—a Victorian or digital-age design—to the Modern experiments of the early 1920s and 1930s. Although most type histories refer to the eighteenth-century developments in type design and manufacture as "modern" (referring specifically to modelling or gradation from thick to thin strokes and flat and unbracketed serifs), in this context the term refers to the birth of the New Typography of the 1920s and the shift toward sans serif type.

The book is at once a style guide to type design and a timeline of the evolutionary path laid down as designers reflected the zeitgeist and worked within the technological framework of their respective times. *Typology* examines how the history of type design and typography has been a confluence of, and sometimes a debate between, a series of dichotomies: art/craft, craft/technology, technology/business, and business/idealism. Throughout the eras when type was cut from wood, cast in lead, and forged on a screen, type design has been a constant process of building on its own historical foundation, which is the essence of this type-ology.

LEFT: EMIGRE #4, *periodical cover, 1985. Designer: Rudy VanderLans.* CENTER: GESTALT, *type specimen, 1989. Designer: Jonathan Hoefler.* RIGHT: WHY? (TIME WARNER), *annual report, 1990. Designer: Kent Hunter.*

"Old Face" types came into being in 1470, when Nicolas Jenson, a Frenchman in Venice, created the first roman (or Humanist) fount in the Venetian style. In 1495, Aldus Manutius launched the Aldine roman tradition with his cut of small capitals paired with lighter lowercase letters (he also designed the first italic typeface). His work influenced sixteenth-century designer Claude Garamond, who fine-tuned a roman that became the standard European type for two centuries. In 1692, French type founder Philippe Granjean cut an intermediate or transitional roman known as *romain du roi* for the printing house of Louis XIII. At that time, *modern* was defined as a technique born of improved technology—stark con-

trast between thick and thin strokes. The first modern face was cut in 1784 at the foundry of Firmin Didot; it was rigid and mechanical compared to the uneven cuts, weights, and shadings of earlier faces. By 1787, both Giambattista Bodoni of Parma, Italy, and J. E. Walbaum in Germany had interpreted Didot. The modern-face roman was introduced to England by John Baskerville and Robert Thorne in 1800, and this face influenced type design throughout the nineteenth century. Many of the subsequent display types were bastardizations of original modern forms, however. The decorated and ornamented display faces of the Victorian era—the mid- to late nineteenth century—cannot be classified as modern in the twentieth-century sense because they are resolutely archaic in relation to the typefaces influenced by progressive design. Modern (with a capital M), which refers to the radical art of the twentieth century, also indicates typefaces stripped of functionless decoration. Nineteenth-century decorative and ornamented wood and metal letters, flamboyantly designed for ephemeral commercial use, prefigured the progressive ideas of functionality and economy that underlie the Modernist ideal, yet they gave rise to the reaction that resulted in change. Victorian type design evolved into proto-Modern type, including a range of eclectic faces from late-nineteenth- and early-twentieth-century Arts and Crafts, Aesthetic, and Art Nouveau movements.

OPPOSITE: COLUMBIA BICYCLE, *poster, c. 1886. Designer unknown.*
ABOVE: MODELES DE LETTRES, *sign painter's specimen, 1884. Designer unknown.*

VICTORIAN ENGLAND

"The first modern faces designed around 1800 and 1810 are charming; neat, rational and witty," wrote Nicolette Gray in *Nineteenth Century Ornamented Types and Title Pages.* "But from that time onwards . . . types grow more and more depressing; the serifs grow longer, the ascenders and descenders grow longer, the letters crowd together." Amid this extraordinary flux in typographic standards emerged a unique style of English Victorian ornamented letter design. Throughout the century, as the concoctions evolved and devolved, it changed the fundamental character of print from comparatively staid to outrageously exuberant. During this time the anonymous progenitors of Victorian styles— type foundry employees—released types that evolved from or were reactions to earlier efforts at making the page exciting, notably the Regency style, which was known for Tuscans characterized by curled, pointed, bifurcated serifs. Some Victorian faces are exaggerations of book types, others are bastardizations of Italian styles. Also common were slab serif Egyptian fonts—developed in response to the fad in Egyptiana stemming from Napoleon's Egyptian campaign—fat faces, and sans serif gothics. Calligraphic traditions were also tapped for the more eccentric forms; decorating the surface of letters with striped and arabesque patterns, as well as open faces, inlines, out-lines, and shadows, was both common and popular. Victorian typeface design runs a wide gamut from uninspired mimicry to confident invention.

1

1. WOMBWELL'S, *broadsheet, c. 1865. Designer unknown.*

2. THE SUPERIOR PRINTER, *trade magazine cover, c. 1870. Designer unknown.*

3. THE AMERICAN MODEL PRINTER, *trade magazine cover, c. 1870. Designer unknown.*

4. THE BRITISH PRINTER, *trade magazine cover, c. 1870. Designer unknown.*

5. SCHILLING & CO, *billhead, c. 1890. Designer unknown.*

6. FANCIE FAYRE, *page of poetry, c. 1880. Designer unknown.*

2

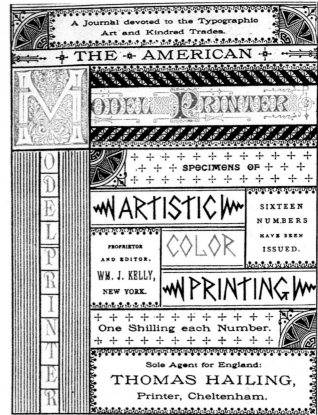

3

4

5

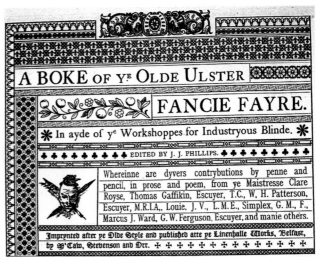

6

VICTORIAN
UNITED STATES

The fashion for outlandish display typefaces was at its peak in the late nineteenth century. It was spurred by the consolidation of many small type foundries into a few large conglomerates with regional outlets. These supplied virtually all of America's commercial job printers for whom advertising was the stock and trade. England was the wellspring of the Victorian style, but widespread piracy and mimicry made hundreds of English faces commonly available in America. Gloriously displayed in trade journal samplers, a panoply of old and new designs were regularly made into wood or metal fonts. Printing and type founding were huge industries meeting the demands of both increased literacy and greater consumerism. Not coincidently, the growth of book and magazine publishing paralleled the explosion of printed advertising, which echoed the widespread availability of new products sold through a growing number of retail merchants. The introduction of jovial and often clumsy letter forms, Tuscans, Gothics, and Egyptians—fat faces, slab serifs, ornamented and curlicue letters, with names like Elephant (with its bulbous body), and Rustic (a novelty face in the shape of wooden logs)—was bizarre, yet attracted attention.

---

7. TYLER PATENT BATTING, *sign, c. 1880. Designer unknown.*

8. UNIVERSAL WRITING BOOK, *book cover, 1892. Designer unknown.*

9. PALM'S PATENT TRANSFER LETTERS, *sign specimen, 1885. Designer unknown.*

10. MRS. S. A. ALLEN'S, *advertisement, c. 1880. Designer unknown.*

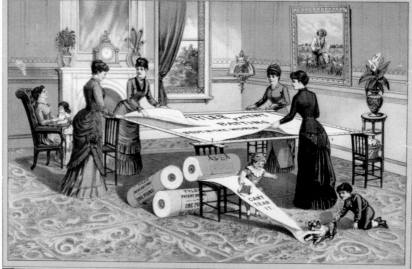

7

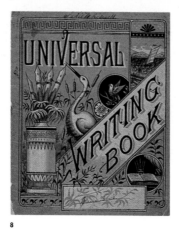

8

9

Novelties in Literature—Music—Literary, Art and Social Gossip—Work Table—Household—
Fall and Winter Fashions—Etc., Etc.

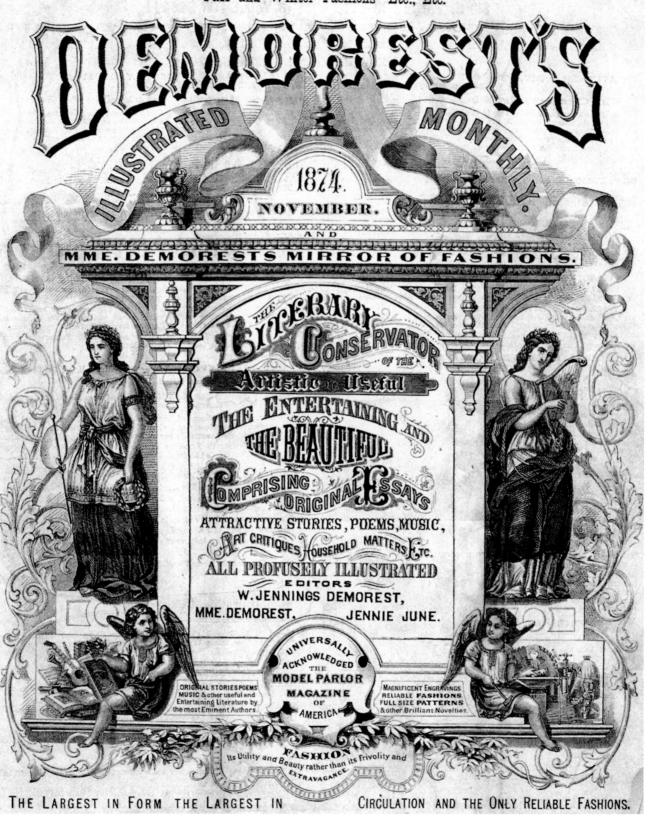

DEMOREST'S

ILLUSTRATED MONTHLY.

1874. NOVEMBER.

AND

MME. DEMORESTS MIRROR OF FASHIONS.

THE LITERARY CONSERVATOR OF THE Artistic & Useful

THE ENTERTAINING AND THE BEAUTIFUL

COMPRISING ORIGINAL ESSAYS

ATTRACTIVE STORIES, POEMS, MUSIC,
ART CRITIQUES HOUSEHOLD MATTERS ETC.

ALL PROFUSELY ILLUSTRATED

EDITORS

W. JENNINGS DEMOREST,
MME. DEMOREST.   JENNIE JUNE.

ORIGINAL STORIES POEMS MUSIC & other useful and Entertaining Literature by the most Eminent Authors.

UNIVERSALLY ACKNOWLEDGED THE MODEL PARLOR MAGAZINE OF AMERICA

MAGNIFICENT ENGRAVINGS RELIABLE FASHIONS FULL SIZE PATTERNS & other Brilliant Novelties.

FASHION
Its Utility and Beauty rather than its Frivolity and EXTRAVAGANCE.

THE LARGEST IN FORM THE LARGEST IN   CIRCULATION AND THE ONLY RELIABLE FASHIONS.

11

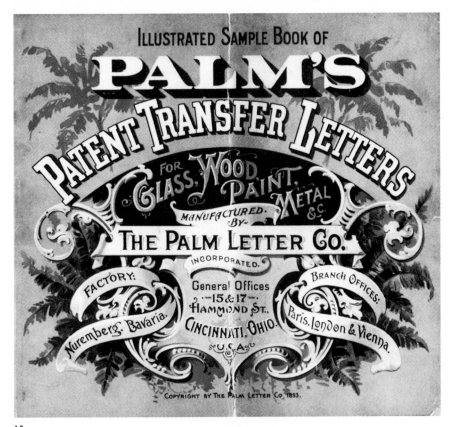

12

13

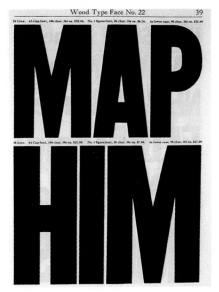

14

15

VICTORIAN
UNITED STATES

Architecture was an influence on both page and type design of the nineteenth century. The term *architectonic* was not merely a metaphor, but a style that appropriated the decorative aspects of Victorian facades and monuments in the same way that these decorations were incorporated in the heavy machinery of the age. Magazine cover illustrations were detailed with filigrees, while the type gave the appearance of letters carved in stone. Considering the cumbersome wood and metal engraving techniques used to create these intricate concoctions, the results are remarkably precise. It appears that precision was a greater virtue than any other aesthetic concern. This was the era when artisans challenged their media at every turn. It was a time when the highest endeavor was to twist and contort the brass metal rules used in page composition to do feats of typographic acrobatics they were never manufactured to do. It was also an age of especially fine draftsmanship, when artists took pride in bringing the most eccentric ideas to life. The Victorian style was not limited to the extraordinary, however. Most job printers did journeyman work with the standard Gothic wood types available, and if they didn't have enough of one font, they mixed in others.

11: DEMOREST'S, *magazine cover, 1874. Designer unknown.*

12. PALM'S, *catalog cover, 1885. Designer unknown.*

13. H. M. SANDERS, *billhead, c. 1890. Designer unknown.*

14-15. WOOD TYPE FACE NO. 22, *specimen sheet, c. 1890. Designer unknown.*

VICTORIAN
FRANCE

While the term *Victorian*, with its reference to the reign of the British Queen, is not exactly an accurate means to categorize French type of this period, the stylistic similarity between England and the Continent is not coincidental. Type and lettering were exportable goods, although because of the weight of metal and wood fonts they were also bulky goods. Despite the existence of key nineteenth-century French foundries, including Firmin Didot and Fonderie Deberny & Cie, that produced original typefaces on their own, one reason that French and English display faces were so similar was piracy. This was a two-way street, of course; the English were not ashamed to claim French originality as their own. The popularity of Egyptian slab serif faces throughout Europe, however, must be credited to a popular fascination in Egyptiana after Napoleon's 1798 campaign and to the subsequent architecture and monuments that sprung up around Paris on this theme. In addition, some of the ornate type designs of this era evolved directly from French Rococo printing from the seventeenth century. French founders developed important transitional and modern faces, but for purposes of commerce (signs and printed matter) small commercial printers and sign painters used exaggerated variations of these faces as well as other decorative motifs. With the advent of new chromolithographic printing technologies, ornate letter forms were given additional carnival-like exuberance by the application of colorful inks that brightened up the printed page.

16

16. EXPOSITION UNIVERSELLE, *book title page, 1855. Designer unknown.*

17-24. MODELES DE LETTRES, *specimen sheets, 1884. Designer unknown.*

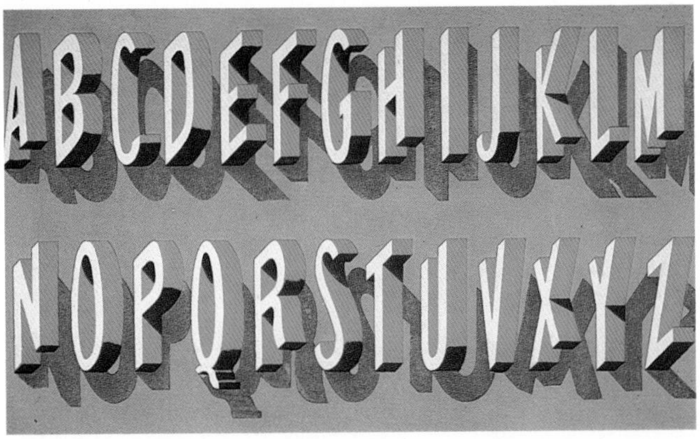

ABCDEFGHIJKLM
NOPQRSTUVXYZ

17

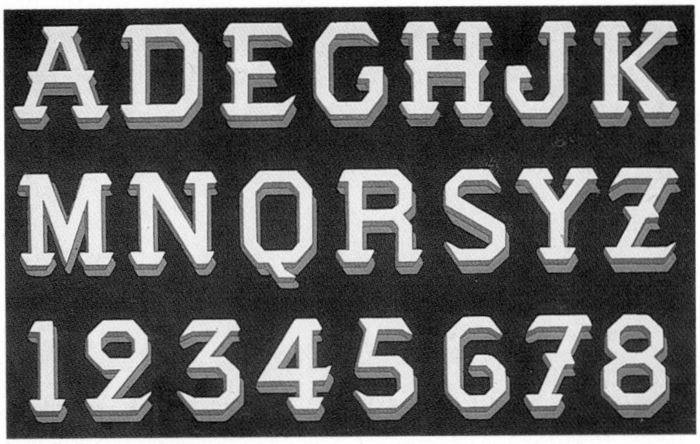

ADEGHJK
MNQRSYZ
12345678

18

MANUEL
DE
PEINTURES.

19

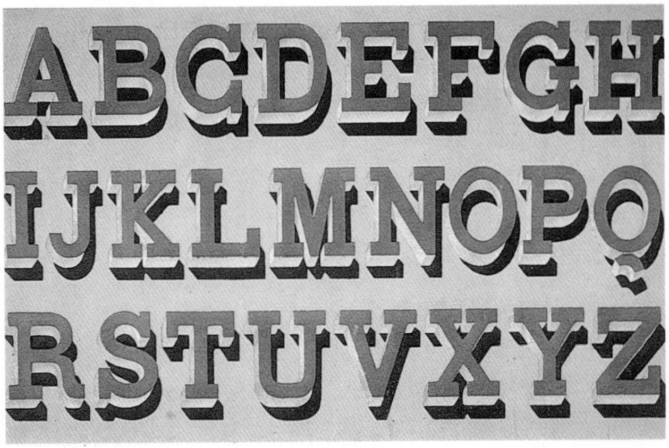

ABCDEFGH
IJKLMNOPQ
RSTUVXYZ

20

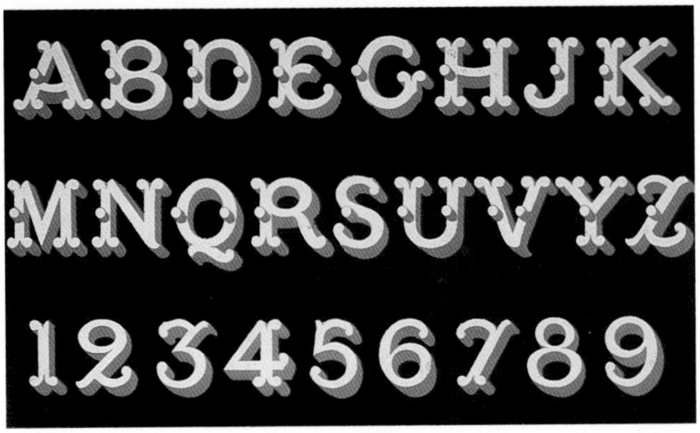

ABDEGHJK
MNQRSUVYZ
123456789

21

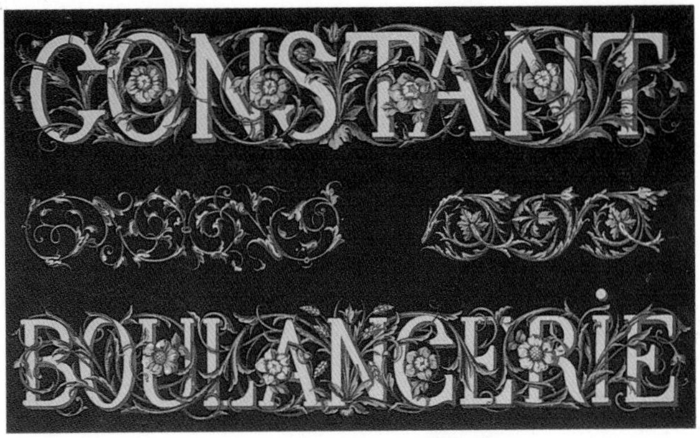

CONSTANT
BOULANGERIE

22

VERNIS
COBALT

23

ABCDEFGH
IJKLMNOPQ
RSTUVXYZ

24

27

25

26

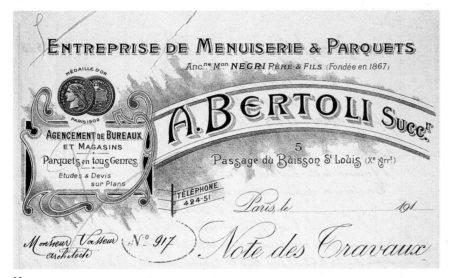

27

28

29

30

31

32

VICTORIAN FRANCE

Business and industry in France grew in leaps and bounds during the late nineteenth century after the transition from monarchy to Republic. The commercial print shops were likewise working overtime, cranking out the posters, broadsheets, and bills that characterized this transitional period in typography. Although type purists argue that this was a time of appallingly gaudy type design and undisciplined composition, it is unfair to compare commercial work with fine book printing, which was the gold standard of type at the time. While technology allowed for relatively large print runs of mass items, it did not assure the same quality that was achieved on small hand-fed printing presses. The fairly large quantity of printing for mass consumption was done quickly on steam presses, but without regard for aesthetic nuances. Bold poster types were designed to grab attention, and job printers cared little about which type families worked well with others, resulting in the many discordances that characterize typographic styles of the day. At the same time, individual job printers were purveyors of the elaborate engraved cartouches that were standard fare for letterheads and commercial design.

25. AU SPÉCULATEUR, *poster, c. 1880. Designer unknown.*

26. A L'OEIL, *poster, c. 1880. Designer unknown.*

27. LA PREVOYANCE, *letterhead, 1890. Designer unknown.*

28. A. BERTOLI, *billhead, c. 1890. Designer unknown.*

29-32. MODELES DE LETTRES, *specimen sheets, 1884. Designer unknown.*

VICTORIAN GERMANY

Blackletter, Germany's national typeface, dates back to the printing of Gutenberg's Mainz bible and Psalters in the fourteenth century. Beginning in the eighteenth century, however, a polarity existed in German printing between the complex, spiky Blackletter (which will be discussed later), and the simpler, crystalline roman, which was symbolic of a much broader schism between *Nationalkultur* and a more worldly view. German Romanticism encouraged a national spirit in German art (as in politics), and proponents attempted to unify all nationally made art, as well as commercial products, through distinctly Germanic mannerisms. Nevertheless, the Victorian aesthetic found its way into, and was welcomed by, German commercial print shops. Much of the quotidian business typography, such as signs and billheads, was a curious mixture of German Blackletter styles (Textura, Schwabacher, and Fraktur) with roman-inspired, decorated letters; some of the specimens of the day also derived from ancient manuscript illuminations and ornate scripts. In addition, type founders and printers imported or pirated many quirky variations of Egyptian and Italian style faces that the very skilled German printers transformed into indigenous-looking design. Germany, which always prided itself on fine-printing traditions, was in the vanguard of stone lithography and chromolithography; thus the look and feel of German Victorian—era type was defined by the velvet softness of the lithographic process.

33

34

35

33. BUSINESS SIGNS, *specimen sheet, 1896. Designer unknown.*

34. PLASTISCHE STEINSCHRIFT, *specimen sheet, c. 1898. Designer unknown.*

35. PLASTISCHE JONISCHE SCHRIFT, *specimen sheet, c. 1898. Designer unknown.*

36-37. ANTIQUA, *specimen sheets, 1896. Designer unknown.*

38-39. SCHRIFTEN ATLAS, *specimen sheets, 1896. Designer: N. Glaise.*

40. INITIAL LETTERS, *medieval style from Schriften Atlas, 1890. Designer unknown.*

36

37

38

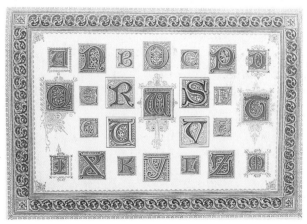

39

40

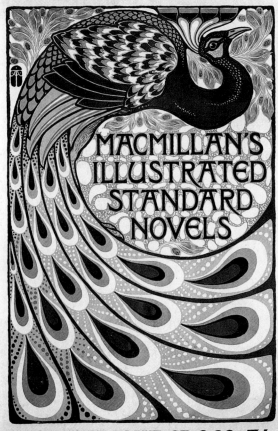

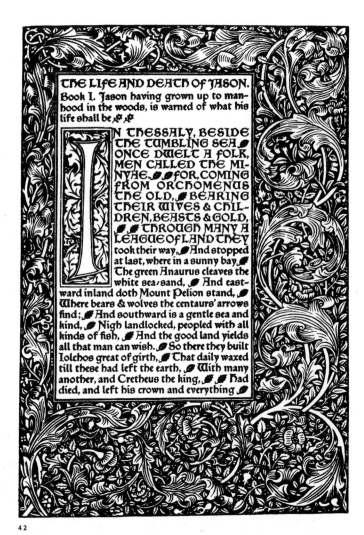

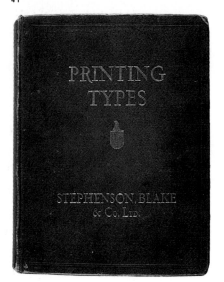

41

42

43

44

45

ARTS AND CRAFTS ENGLAND

The Arts and Crafts movement began in England in the 1880s through groups like the Century Guild, the Arts and Crafts Society, and the Art-Worker's Guild and was promoted in the journal *The Century Guild Hobby Horse*. This publication was devoted to inspiring a higher quality in the book arts. The movement sought to return enfeebled British crafts to a state of excellence and wed all the fine and applied arts. The movement had many voices until it ostensibly came under the leadership of William Morris, poet and polymath designer, whose Kelmscott Press (founded in 1891) became the vanguard of this medieval-inspired, anti-Victorian sensibility. Influenced by John Ruskin's celebration of Gothic architecture as the only pure form, and later by book designer Sir Emery Walker at a lecture on the history of type, Morris designed his own Golden Type in 1890 and fervently sought the total reformation of printing types. Morris and his kindred spirits despised the dehumanizing effects of Victorian industrialism and attempted to establish an alternative aesthetic based on quality handwork. In recalling the past, Morris argued for greater control over the direct means of production, as well as attention to aesthetic standards. In England, some Arts and Crafts members moved toward Art Nouveau, others toward a purist aesthetic movement.

46. H. W. CASLON & CO., *advertisement, c. 1890. Designer unknown.*

47. R. MARDEN & CO., *letterhead, c. 1900. Designer: W. H. Smith.*

48. WRENS CITY CHURCHES, *book cover, 1883. Designer: A. H. Mackmurdo.*

ARTS AND CRAFTS
UNITED STATES

The standards of commercial printing in the United States fluctuated as much as in England, if not more, owing to an incomparable demand for nationwide advertising. Throughout the country, small print shops produced vast quantities of typeset material, routinely following the styles and techniques passed along in the specimen books produced by large foundries. Not all job printers were created equal, however, and both talent and expertise varied. Influenced by England's Arts and Crafts movement, William Morris, and historicism itself, and a few so-called "fine" printers working "private" presses, ventured into areas that bucked convention and ultimately set new standards for type design and composition. The American Arts and Crafts movement emerged through small workshops that, in the Morris tradition, wed different applied arts together, including furniture, textiles, and printing. Handicrafts, as opposed to machine production, was the foremost virtue; but in the realm of typography, with the notable exception of hand-set and hand-printed broadsheets and limited editions, the steam-powered printing press and Monotype and Linotype machines were irrefutable facts of life. Given the requisites of the marketplace, commercial founders and designers raised the level of quality by applying the spirit, if not the letter, of the Arts and Crafts.

49-52. AMERICAN TYPE FOUNDERS CO. DESK BOOK, *type specimens, 1905.*

53. WHEN HEARTS ARE TRUMPS, *book jacket/poster, 1894. Designer: Will Bradley.*

49

50

51

52

53

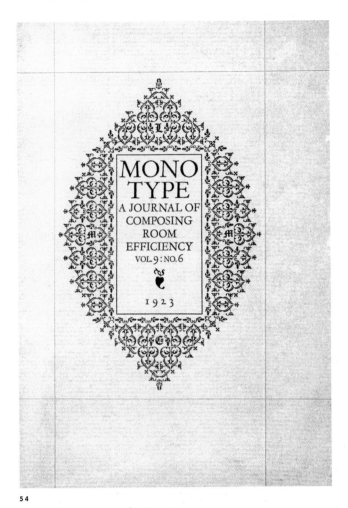

54

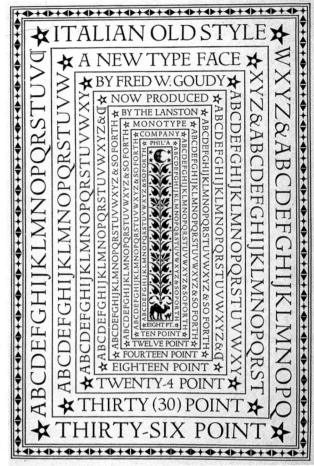

55

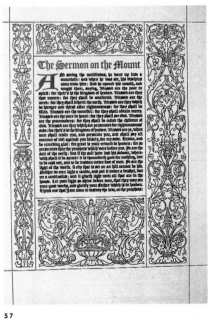

56

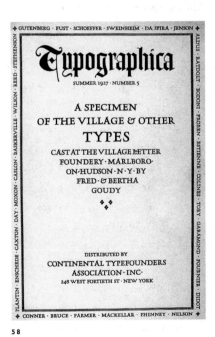

57

58

---

54. MONTOYPE, *periodical cover, 1923.*
Designer: Bruce Rogers.

55. ITALIAN OLD STYLE, *specimen sheet,*
1924. Type designer: Frederic Goudy;
specimen designer: Bruce Rogers.

56. MODERN TYPE DISPLAY, *book cover,*
1920. Designer: J. L. Frazier.

57. THE SERMON ON THE MOUNT,
book page, 1919. Designer: John Henry
Nash.

58. TYPOGRAPHICA, *periodical cover,*
1927. Designer: Frederic Goudy.

59

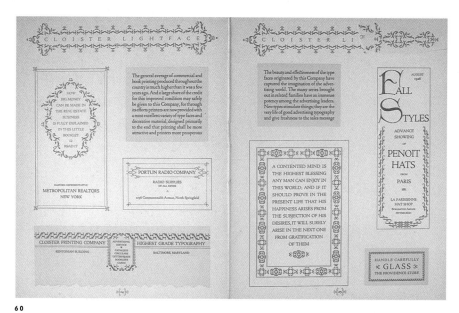

60

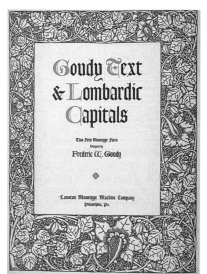

61

62

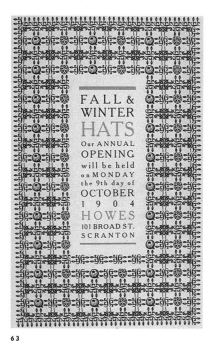

63

64

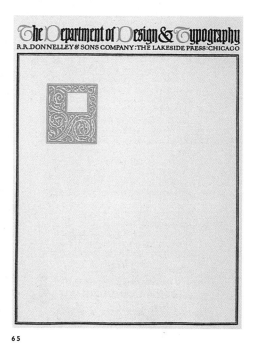

65

66

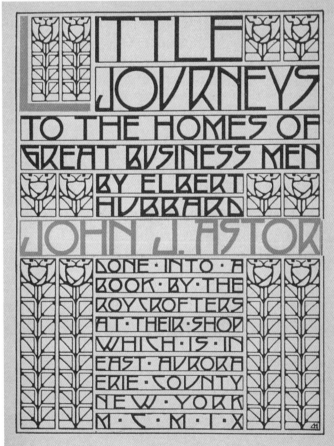

67

ARTS AND CRAFTS
UNITED STATES

Around the late 1890s, the Aesthetic Movement emerged, a loose-knit group of "book builders" and typographers whose goal was to revive historical models for contemporary application. They reprised Old Style faces, including Italians, Gothics, and Caslons, as well as Moderns. Decoration was adopted that revisited both medieval and rococo sensibilities, and this continued well into the 1920s. Some Morris acolytes attempted to recreate the guild system. Elbert Hubbard established a crafts community called the Roycrofters in East Aurora, New York, where he published books using custom typefaces and ornament. His output did not entirely mimic the Kelmscott Press, and he was criticized for a lack of fealty. Commerce was of growing importance, and most type designers attempted to reform commercial printing rather than retire into craft utopias. While designers and printers like Will Bradley, Frederic Goudy, Bruce Rogers, and D. B. Updike produced the finest printed matter through chap books and limited editions, they also mainstreamed their wares.

59-60. THE PACKARD SERIES, *specimen sheet, 1913. Type designers: Oswald Cooper/Morris Fuller Benton.*

61-62. GOUDY TEXT & LOMBARDIC CAPITALS, *specimen sheet, 1928. Type designer: Frederic Goudy.*

63-64. AMERICAN CHAP-BOOK, *periodical pages, 1904. Designer: Will Bradley.*

65. THE DEPARTMENT OF DESIGN & TYPOGRAPHY, *letterhead, 1900. Designer: Paul Ressinger.*

66. THE BOY FROM MISSOURI VALLEY, *booklet cover, 1909. Designer: Elbert Hubbard.*

67. LITTLE JOURNEYS, *booklet cover, 1904. Type designer: Dard Hunter.*

ARTS AND CRAFTS
GERMANY

Revivalism found German adherents at the turn of the century and for a decade thereafter. German printers had always shown interest in their traditions and the broader history of printing, but in the period that paralleled the introduction of *Jugendstil* (Art Nouveau), a schism arose between those who owed allegiance to the past and those who celebrated the present. Although in Germany the handicraft sensibility was not officially termed Arts and Crafts, the aesthetics were indeed similar. There was a move to revive typefaces in the Italian style while modernizing the Blackletter. Medieval references were present in decorative letterforms, but new serif, sans serif, and swash alphabets were also developed for commercial type foundries. German types of this period were based on brush and woodcut lettering; indeed much of the type was actually hand-lettered and cut as faces afterward. F. H. Emcke was one of the leaders of the historicist school; he acknowledged the Gothic tradition and also pushed the boundaries of tradition with precisionist decorative work. Rudolf Koch was also a typographic revivalist who worked within the existing parameters of the Gothic. He ventured beyond tradition with his proto-Modern sans serif, Kabel. The key to German typography of the era was balance, while symmetry was adhered to as the principal virtue.

68. INSEL-ALMANACH, *cover, 1909. Designer: F. H. Emcke.*

69-70. ZELTINGER/GEISENHEIMER, *business cards, 1911. Designer: F. H. Emcke.*

71. INITIALS, *specimen, c. 1905.*

68

69

70

71

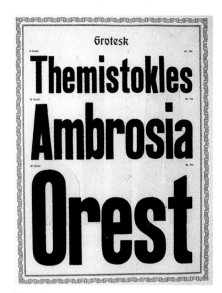

72

73

74

75

76

72-74. SCHRIFTPROBEN, *type specimens (Koch Schrift and Grotesk), c. 1905. Designer unknown.*

75. SCHRIFTEN NEBST ZIERAT, *type catalog, 1909. Designer unknown.*

76. FREIE INTIALEN AND MAGERE KLEUKENS INITALEN, *type specimens, 1909. Designer(s) unknown.*

ART NOUVEAU
GERMANY

Walter Crane, the English Arts and Crafts illustrator/designer, called Art Nouveau "That strange decorative disease." In fact, Art Nouveau was a stylistic revolution in all the applied arts, characterized by what was described as "floreated madness" owing to the exotic motifs inspired by nature. In books and periodicals, the tendency for excessive naturalist decorative borders with strangling stems and tendrils was the modern alternative to the rococo indulgences of a previous age. Like a weed, Art Nouveau took hold throughout Europe, with each participating nation contributing a particular indigenous variation. It was known as *Jugendstil* (or "youth style") in Germany, where it symbolized a paradigm shift in social and cultural attitudes. It was *Le Style Moderne* in France, *Sezessionstil* in Austria and East Europe, *Stile Liberty* (and *Stile Inglese*) in Italy, *Modernista* in Spain, and Art Nouveau—now the most commonly used term—in England and the United States. Art Nouveau was forged in the crucible of industrial flux—the seismic shifts as Europe became modern—and its adherents were at once reacting against, yet cognizant of, the impact of machinery on their cultures. As an alternative to the Victorian need to hide manufactured wares, Art Nouveau was based on fealty to organic structure, albeit an abstraction of nature.

77. CERMOOS, *advertisement, c. 1900. Designer unknown.*

78. H. GOTTWICK, *advertisement, c. 1900. Designer unknown.*

79. GEZEICHNETE SCHRIFTEN, *alphabet, c. 1898. Designer: Peter Schnorr.*

77

78

ABCD
EFGH
IJKLMN
OPQR
SUTD
WXYZ

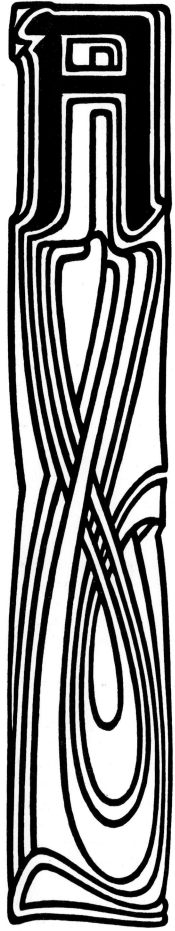

A B C D E F G H I J K
L M N O P Q R S T U

81

A B C D E F G H I J K L
M N O P Q R S T U V W

82

Propaganda   Preise nach Klasse F

Theater 3 Xanten
No. 51414. 8 Cicero   No. 51416. 10 Cicero

Geographie 5
No. 51418. 12 Cicero

Dresden 7
No. 51422. 16 Cicero

Nachrufs
No. 51423. 18 Cicero

J. G. Schelter & Giesecke in Leipzig

80   83

42

TYPES FOR THE GOLD BLOCKING PRESS

TIP-TOP

Schrift Nr. 2740	Ziffern Nr. 2740	Anwendung
OLIVER TWIST	1234567890	JULIUS CÄSAR
Initialen Nr. 2745	Initials Nr. 2745	Iniciales Nr. 2745
BERLIN	FLORENZ	GEROLSTEIN
Schrift Nr. 2741	Chiffres Nr. 2741	Combinaison
HERKULES	12345678	OMPHALE
Initialen Nr. 2746	Schrift Nr. 2743	Initials Nr. 2746
VISTA	IBSEN	DUKTUS
Schrift Nr. 2742	Figures Nr. 2742	Combination
ANHALT	123456	DESSAU
Initialen Nr. 2747	Schrift Nr. 2744	Iniziali Nr. 2747
PER	DIVA	SIRE

Number . .	2740	2741	2742	2743	2744	Number . .	2745	2746	2747
105 Letters Mark	27.—	30.—	35.—	45.—	55.—	25 Initials Mark	20.—	30.—	40.—
30 Figures Mark	7.50	9.—	10.50	13.50	16.50	1 Initial Mark	1.—	1.50	2.—

84

**ABCDEFGHIJKL
MNOPQRSTUVW
123456·XYZ·7890**

85

---

80. INITIAL, *specimen, c. 1886. Type designer: Peter Behrens.*

81. SIEGFRIED, *alphabet, c. 1900. Type designer: Wilhelm Woellmer.*

82. EDEL GOTISCHE, *alphabet, c. 1900. Type designer unknown.*

83. PROPAGANDA, *type specimen, 1897. Type designer unknown.*

84. TIP-TOP, *specimen, 1900. Type designer unknown.*

85. BOCKLIN, *alphabet, c. 1900. Type designer: Arnold Bocklin.*

ART NOUVEAU
GERMANY

The beginning of *Jugendstil* in 1896 was marked by the publication of the magazine *Jugend* (Youth), which is credited with giving its name to the movement. *Jugend* was an art, culture, and humor periodical aimed at those characterized by its title—the younger generation of "bohemians"—and its mission was to capture German art from the academics and romantics and inject it with a new vitality. This was the era of unification, when autonomous German states and principalities became one nation. *Jugendstil* was a symbol, although not an altogether natural outgrowth, of this otherwise conservative rise of nationalism. *Jugend* proffered a contentious editorial policy, often at odds with authority (i.e., the Kaiser), that proposed changes in political and social conventions that gave preference to the ruling classes. Likewise, graphically it vehemently challenged the strictures of sanctioned art. Although *Jugend's* text type was usually the archaic Blackletter, the most common German text, its display lettering conformed to no such bounds. Covers were colorful with outrageous (for the times) illustrations of unromantic themes; the *Jugend* logo changed with each issue, often appearing in sinuous, barely legible letterforms. As the lettering became increasingly more eccentric, the movement's designers sought additional opportunities to be outrageous. The most fervent *Jugendstil* proponents were not concerned with being safe, but in driving the formal properties of type and image as far from convention as the means at their disposal allowed.

43

A R T   N O U V E A U
G E R M A N Y

Art Nouveau artists were noted for their erotic obsessions, which were evident in the plague of nymphs and nymphets found in decorative borders, illuminated typefaces, and illustrations, but despite its rarefaction and decadence which was nourished by a fairly generous dose of religious mysticism, Art Nouveau was enthusiastically accepted as a popular style among the bourgeoisie. German *Jugendstil* was never as eccentric as that practiced in other nations, and it was also quicker to dissipate. During the decade that it was in demand, however, businesses adopted the graphics as tools of contemporary commercial style whether or not the approach was appropriate to their respective products or services. *Jugendstil* graphics signified a time rather than a function—any object could be given the veneer and thus appear modern—but there was a trick to making *Jugendstil* work. Type, ornament, and decorative illustration were components of an entire aesthetic and had to be used in tandem with other design materials. The *Jugendstil* gestalt was tied to the combination of a variety of different graphic accoutrements, from borders to rules. Ultimately, *Jugendstil* gave credence to the fact that type was not a static medium.

---

86. VERLAG MODERNE, *advertisement, c. 1910. Designer: Eugen Gradl.*

87. ODOL, *advertisement, c. 1908. Designer: G. M. Ellwood.*

88. OTTO GOTHA, *advertisement, c. 1900. Designer: George Auriol.*

89. RESTAURANT BAHNHOF, *advertisement, c. 1910. Designer: J. V. Cissarz.*

90. INITIALS, *type specimen, c. 1891. Type designer: Peter Behrens.*

86

87

Otto
Gotha
Berlin
Kiel

88

RESTAURANT
BAHNHOF
STUTTGART

FRÜHSTÜCK
DINERS
SOUPERS
BELEGTE
BRÖDCHEN

89

90

45

ART NOUVEAU
FRANCE

Paris is erroneously assumed to be the birthplace of Art Nouveau (*Le style moderne* or *style nouveau*), but it was actually a recipient—one of the many locales where the "new wave" landed as it washed over Europe. The furniture and glass designer Emil Gallé, of Nancy, introduced France to Art Nouveau in 1888 after returning from England, and the impresario Sigfried Bing, who opened a shop called Art Nouveau, gave Paris its first taste. Since Paris was a mecca for artists from all over Europe, the foreign-born practitioners of the pan-European style contributed as much to what became the French dialect as did the native-born. During the late nineteenth century, Paris was awash with design exuberance. Posters filled the streets with colorful lithographic renderings, and the hand-lettered headlines on these *affiche* developed into a style of French type that conformed to the new architecture, furniture, textiles, and other designs. French *affichistes* Jules Cheret and Henri Toulouse-Lautrec and the Czech Alphonse Mucha helped define the obsessive French style. Type was manufactured to serve the huge needs of commerce. Almost immediately after an artist concocted a lettering style for a poster, a foundry, such as the famous Fonderie Deberny & Cie, would manufacture a complete design of all letters and ornaments for commercial use. Sometimes the original designer was employed—George Auriol, the quintessential Art Nouveau designer, designed his own—while other times the unprotected work was simply appropriated.

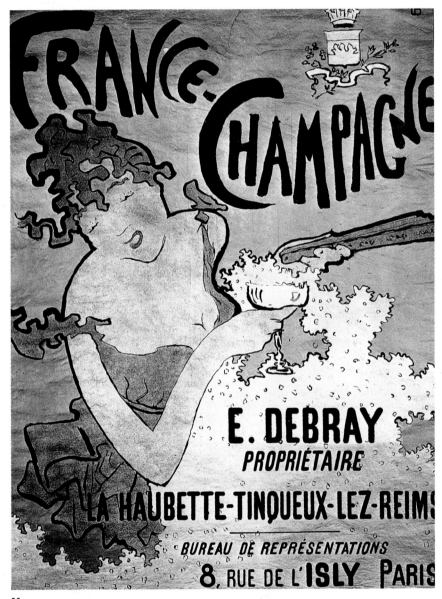

91

92

91. ARTISTÉ, *alphabet, 1890. Type designer unknown.*

92. FRANCE-CHAMPAGNE, *poster, 1881. Designer: Pierre Bonnard.*

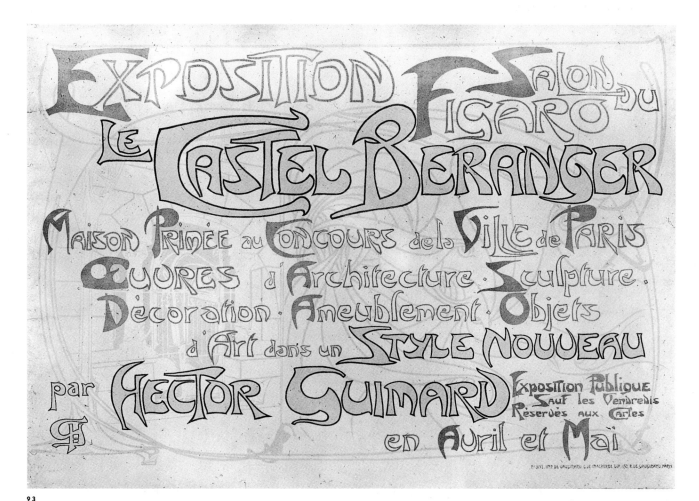

93

94

95

96

93. EXPOSITION LE CASTEL BERANGER,
poster, 1900. Designer: Hector Guimard.

94-96. LETTRES MODERNES, *from
Fonderie Deberny & Cie catalog, c. 1891.*

L'INTÉRIEUR MODERNE

MEUBLES
MENUISERIE
DÉCORATION
P. BEC & DIOT
SUCCESSEURS

97

98

ABCDEFGHIJKLMNOP
ab · QRSTUVWXYZ · cd
: efghijklmnopqrstuvwxyz :

99

ABCDEFGHIJKLM
NOPQRSTUVWXYZ
1234567890

100

ABCDEFGHIJKLM
NOPQRSTUVWX
abcde · yz · fghikl

101

ABCDEFGHIJKLMN
OPQRSTUVWXYZ
abcdefghijklmnopqr
stuv · GOUNOD · wxyz

102

ART NOUVEAU FRANCE

French Art Nouveau initially changed the look and manufacture of furniture and textiles before it influenced printing and graphic design. The two leading "schools," in Nancy and Paris, had differing levels of stylistic intensity—the former was more ostentatious; the latter was comparatively austere. The style was introduced in architecture in Paris through the work of Hector Guimard, the designer of Metro stations (only his entry signs remain). Guimard's decorative fantasies took Art Nouveau into new realms of eccentricity and inspired others to push the bounds of printing ornament and type design. He was a symbolist, and his decorative designs expressed a spiritual mood while serving a utilitarian function. He believed that ornament should be abstract, but nevertheless rooted in the design of nature. Printer's ornaments—inextricably wedded to the composition of all type and lettering—were likewise designed to give the page both functional and spiritual depth. In practice, Art Nouveau alphabets evoked a sense of contemporaneity in common product advertisements. The style twisted itself around all kinds of commercial printed matter.

97. L'INTÉRIEUR MODERNE, *advertisement, c. 1910. Designer unknown.*

98. MODES DE SYLVIE ROSE, *advertisement, 1895. Designer: George Auriol.*

99. GLORIA, *alphabet, c. 1895. Type designer unknown.*

100. METROPOLITAINES, *alphabet, c. 1895. Type designer unknown.*

101. HERCULES, *alphabet, c. 1895. Type designer unknown.*

102. SECESSION, *alphabet, c. 1895. Type designer unknown.*

103

104

DE RECLAME

4ᴰᴱ JAAR Nº 2 — FEBRUARI 1925

HET GOEDE MIDDEL OP DEN JUISTEN TIJD

MAAND —BLAD—
VOOR RECLAME EN
RECLAME·KUNST

J.M. HARTKAMP

105

ABCDEFGHIKLV
MNJOPRSTUW

106

ABCDEFGHIJK
LMNOPQRSTUV
MAG OWXYZZ RAW

107

ABCDEFGHIJKLM
NOIPRSTUVWX

108

ADSMNPKSV
HZLFIREBC

109

ART NOUVEAU
THE NETHERLANDS

110

While the Netherlands was not a wellspring of Art Nouveau glass, furniture, textiles, or architecture, its designers did make a significant national contribution to type and graphic design. As in France, Dutch designers embraced the formal and symbolic ideas that infused Post-impressionism and the Japanese woodblock print. In addition to these foreign influences, however, the Dutch were interested in clearly defined geometric planes and a degree of symmetry, not unlike the topography of the small country itself. Making order out of chaos was the goal of the serious designer. Compared to the French, Dutch typographic design was a model of restraint, yet still decidedly decorative in the manner of *Jugendstil*, which was perhaps its closest cousin. Many of the popular alphabets employed by job printers echoed (if not mimicked) designs from France and Germany, although the Dutch did not embrace the spiky German gothics. The characteristic stiffness has a connection with the woodcut medium, which was widely used for posters and other graphics; the more sinuous compositions were done as lithographs. The majority of Dutch display type was designed for large-scale reproduction and was based on the poster lettering of the day. Jan Toorop was one of the leading Art Nouveau stylists; his work, which was influenced by French posters and Japanese graphics, was the quintessence of curvilinear expression. As its legacy, Dutch type designers developed exquisite fantasy alphabets that pervaded the visual environment of the day.

103. PROGRAMMA CONCERTGEBOUW, *program cover, c. 1922. Designer: R. N. Roland Holst.*

104. DE TOEGEPASTE KUNSTEN IN NEDERLAND, *book cover, 1924. Designers: W. L. and J. Brusse.*

105. DE RECLAME, *magazine cover, 1925. Designer: J. M. Hartkamp.*

106-109. UNTITLED ALPHABETS, *specimens, 1915. Type designer: J. H. Kaemmerer.*

110. ARNHEM, *poster, 1907. Designer: Dan Hoeksema.*

ART NOUVEAU
THE NETHERLANDS

Dutch Art Nouveau was characterized by France's curvilinear design motifs yet with a distinctive hard rectilinear edge. At the turn of the century, businesses wanted whatever support they could get from advertising specialists to push goods and services into the public's homes. Mammoth type specimen books with a wide array of eye-catching typographical variations were produced and distributed to commercial job printers. Mostly designed by anonymous foundry draftsmen, the results ran the gamut from the typical style of European Art Nouveau imports to arcane original designs that pushed the boundaries of the style into even more eccentric realms. These typographic novelties frequently turned up in newspaper and periodical advertisements and were also commonly used for wood and painted-glass store signs. New photographic reproduction methods made it possible to achieve unprecedented effects, including the layering of one type over another to produce a third face (not unlike what is accomplished today on the computer). The unstoppable outrageousness of these designs provoked critics to decry typographic standards—and forced traditional designers to find more austere alternatives. But the exuberance of the Art Nouveau–influenced period resulted in some fascinating type and typography.

111

112

111. UW MODE TIJDSCHRIFT, *poster,
1904. Designer unknown.*

112. ALPHABET, *specimen, c. 1900. Type
designer unknown.*

113-116. LETTERING, *specimen
sheets. c. 1910. Type designer unknown.*

RESTAURANT · HÔTEL · CAFÉ

MAISON DUCATER

BOUWKUNDIG BUREAU · ROMAN · TRUSCH

DEUKALION

113

FIJNE BORDEAUX 18-87

BOEKDRUKKUNST

DRENTHE · DRESDEN

BODEGA 22 OPORTO · EKKOBU · DE GEKROONDE W

114

A · BROOD-KOEK EN · N
18 BANKET 36
N · BAKKERIJ · O

NEDERLAND · HÔTEL

CIGAREN TABAK CHOCOLADE

115

GLADIATOR
STAATSLIEN
HANOVER.
TABLEAUX
MASTER
WIKEND
TIMOTHEÜS
COSTUMES

116

53

117

118

119

120

121

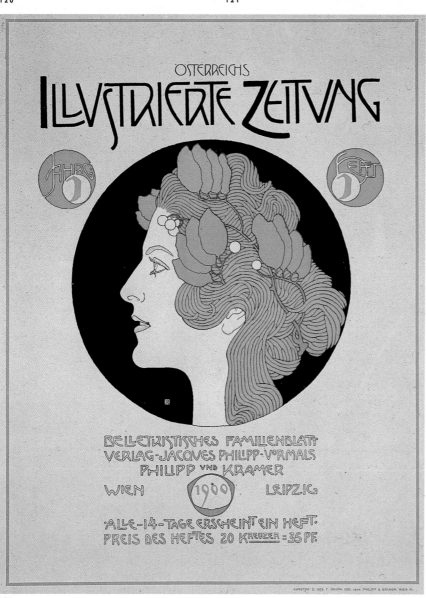

122

ART NOUVEAU AUSTRIA

In Austria, Art Nouveau was synthesized into the Vienna Secession (*Sezession*), founded by a group of architects led by Otto Wagner, Josef Hoffman, and Joseph Olbrich. Influenced by the Glasgow School, Secessionist ornamental motif was based largely on squares and rectangles but tied together through whiplash curves. Hoffman was a book illustrator who developed decorations along these lines and proffered the idea that all forms of design—architectural, interior, furniture, and graphic—complement one another through shared decorative devices. The typography of the Viennese Secession was therefore somewhat blockier than its counterparts elsewhere in Art Nouveau–inspired Europe. The first exhibition of the group took place in 1898 in Vienna where other key Secessionists, including architect and furniture designer Adolf Loos and textile and graphic designer Kolo Moser, showed their wares. The large square periodical *Ver Sacrum* (The Spring) promoted the Secessionist ideas and exhibited the ornament and type styles associated with the group. Some covers were austere, with simple illustration and unembellished sans serif lettering; others were suitably eccentric. The Wiener Werkstätte (Vienna Workshop) was the commercial arm of the design movement. Its diverse graphic design included hard-edged woodcut mannerisms that prefigure German Expressionism.

117. KUNSTSCHAU, *poster, 1908. Designer: Oskar Kokoschka.*

118. DIE FLÄCHE 1, *type specimen, 1900. Type designer: Bruno Seuchter.*

119. BEETHOVEN HAUSER, *catalog cover, c. 1910. Designer: Carl Moll.*

120–121. VER SACRUM, *magazine pages, 1898. Designer: Kolo Moser.*

122. ILLUSTIERTE ZEITUNG, *periodical cover, 1900. Designer: Kolo Moser.*

BLACKLETTER

Blackletter is the umbrella term for the spiky German type genre that includes Textura, Rotunda, Fraktur and Schwabacher and is the direct descendent of Gutenberg's first printing types used in his 42-line Bible of 1455. In subsequent years, the face was revised and refined by printers and founders in German-speaking countries. Fraktur, for example, was developed as a chancery face during the reign of Maximilian I. The primary characteristics of all the variations are the broken curves and the spiky ascenders and descenders of most letters. Blackletter was adopted as the Teutonic typeface and it is arguably better suited to the German language. The schism between Roman (or *Antiqua*, as it is known in Germany) and Blackletter was more than an aesthetic disagreement; it was a deep division between romanticism and rationalism—the letterform is the repository of centuries of cultural strife. Critics argued that Blackletter was an abhorrent monstrosity; adherents said it embodied the Gothic notion of the infinite. Ultimately, it was one of the pre-eminent symbols of German unity and nationalism. Whatever the underpinning, it remained a commonly used alphabet well into the 1920s, when Modern typefaces made inroads. After 1933, the Nazis reclaimed it as the German Letter, until it was branded *Judenletteren* because complaints about its readability reached Nazi officials.

123. MODERNE SCHRIFTEN IN HOLZ, *specimen cover (Schelter & Giecerke Foundry), c. 1920. Designer unknown.*

124. GOTISCHE, *alphabet, c. 1900. Type designer unknown.*

125

126

127

128

129

---

125. TYPOGRAPHISCHE MITTEILUNGEN, *periodical cover, 1925. Designer unknown.*

126. DAS GRÖSHERE DEUTSCHLAND, *periodical cover, 1915. Designer: Lucian Bernhard.*

127. KRAFTIGE SALZMANN FRAKTUR, *type specimen, c. 1905. Type designer unknown.*

128. TYPOGRAPHISCHE MITTEILUNGEN, *periodical cover, 1922. Designer unknown.*

129. WYMIR, *type specimen, c. 1905. Type designer unknown.*

E A R L Y M O D E R N

After the turn of the century, graphic design underwent the first of many major twentieth-century shifts in both form and practice. Advances in technology led to changes in methods of mass communication. America and Europe became more consumer-driven and advertising loomed as an important cultural force. Since at this time print (newspapers, magazines, posters) was the primary means of communicating to the masses, considerable effort was made to improve the medium; therefore progress in the design, manufacture, and distribution of typefaces was paramount. With increased traffic on city streets, strategic locations along them for selling messages were used for advertising, and the marriage of type and image was an invaluable tool in its success. More locations resulted in increased messages and greater competition for the public's attention. The elaborate and eccentric display typefaces in the Art Nouveau style quickly became ineffectual in the cluttered urban landscapes. An alternative advertising style was required to simplify, clarify, and distinguish. The most popular new method, the *Sachplakat*, or object poster, began in Germany around 1906, with the

first poster designed by Lucian Bernhard for Preister Match company. It was characterized by a stark image and bold block lettering combined into a single iconographic representation of the product or idea. The block type that developed during this period was rooted in old Gothic and script traditions, but the faces were used in a more reductive way. *Sachplakat* was not the only early-modern method that challenged the status quo, however. Radical change occurred in the separate and distinct arenas of commerce and art, but art had an even greater impact on twentieth-century type. German Expressionism and Dada redefined the function of typography. Type created by the latter was primitively cut from wood; that produced by the former was a jumbled assortment of typecase pieces. Although neither movement produced commercial faces, they influenced both experimental and commercial type design.

OPPOSITE: MODERNE DRUCKSACHEN, *printer's advertisement, c. 1919. Designer: Richard Erdmann Schmidt.*
ABOVE: DIE LO SCHRIFTEN, *type specimen (H. Berthold, A.G.), c. 1912. Type designer: Louis Oppenheim.*

130

131

132

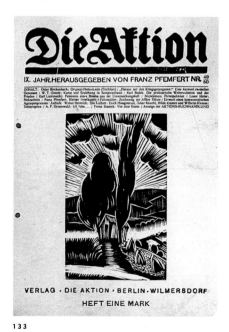

133

130. AN DIE LATERNE (TO THE LAMP-POST), *poster, 1919. Designer unknown.*

131. DER STURM (THE STORM), *poster 1919. Designer: Oskar Kokoschka.*

132. DER WEG (THE WAY), *periodical cover, 1919. Designer: F. Schaefler.*

133. DIE AKTION (ACTION), *periodical cover, 1923. Designer unknown.*

134. EXPRESSIONISMUS: DIE KUNST-WENDE, *catalog cover, 1918. Designer: Wilhelm Wauer.*

135. KG BRÜCKE (THE BRIDGE), *catalog cover, c. 1919. Designer: E. L. Kirchner.*

134

135

EXPRESSIONISM

German Expressionism, founded in 1905, was a movement of rebellious painters repudiating academic strictures. Two Expressionist groups emerged, Die Brücke in 1905 and Der Blaue Reiter in 1911—the former was interested in figuration and the latter in abstraction. Fauvist color influenced both. They mounted exhibitions and produced publications opposed to the tenets of classical beauty. The offspring of their collective radicalism was a visual language based on primitive iconography, including African totems and masks; the woodcut was their medium for unlocking hidden emotions. Deformation of the figure was used to heighten the level of expression. Influenced to a great extent by the polemical graphics published in the satiric journals *Jugend* and *Simplicissimus*, Expressionists found a graphic means to communicate their raw emotions. Prior to World War I, Expressionism attacked convention in metaphysical terms. By 1918, following the November revolution that brought the Weimar Republic to war-ravaged Imperial Germany, the movement became fervently political, allying itself with Socialist and Communist parties. Expressionists broke into factions, such as Die Novembergruppe, which produced propaganda in the battle against right-wing reaction. The postwar Expressionists introduced rigid wood-cut lettering that gave the style its force. The letters grew out of the unforgiving wood medium. The Expressionists did not produce commercial typefaces, but they influenced others even after the movement ended around 1922.

SACHPLAKAT

The *Sachplakat* (object poster) is a distinctly German invention. A reaction to the excesses of Art Nouveau, this minimalist poster genre was founded by Lucian Bernhard and promoted by Ernest Growald in 1906 as a method of advertising products on the increasingly cluttered Berlin poster hoardings. *Sachplakat* is the reduction of a selling message to a minimum number of elements—usually the product, a logo or trademark, and a bold line(s) of type, often in hand-drawn block letters. This method, which was practiced by designers of the Berliner Plakat who were featured in the magazine *Das Plakat*, was championed by the leading German foundries, who rushed original and copied versions of the block letters into production. Although the young Bernhard did not fancy himself a type designer per se, when he saw that his distinctive lettering had been made into a typeface, he decided to enter the business himself. He gave his name to many faces issued by the Flinsch and Bauer type foundries. Another key proponent of this approach, Louis Oppenheim, was compelled to protect his original lettering by designing typefaces for H. Berthold & Co. The typefaces Bernhard, Oppenheim, and others created for advertising prior to World War I were not entirely Modern. Although some were sans serif, others were based on Blackletter and roman scripts. The typical *Sachplakat* faces were bold and often expanded, and included small fat serifs.

136

137

138

139

136. RARITÄT, *poster, c. 1920. Designer: O. W. Hadank.*

137-139. GEG, *posters, c. 1910–12. Designer: Lucian Bernhard.*

140

141

142

143

144

145

140. BERNHARD BLOCK, *type specimen,*
c. 1912. Type designer: Lucian Bernhard.

141. LO KURSIV, *type specimen,*
c. 1912. Type designer: Louis Oppenheim.

142. MODELL D, *advertisement using*
Bernhard Block. c. 1910.

143. DIE LO SCHRIFTEN, *type*
specimen, c. 1912. Type Designer:
Louis Oppenheim.

144. KURBEL PUMPEN, *advertisement*
using Lo Schriften, c. 1910.

145. LO SCHRIFT IN HOLZ, *type speci-*
men, c. 1912. Type designer: Louis
Oppenheim.

Dara geht ins Hotel.

Ein Stück aus dem Roman „Darka ze sich retten" von W. Winnitschenko. Hier veröffentlicht, weil der Roman dieses Kleinrussen, der aus dem Arbeiter ... hervorgegangen ist, bei aller grob zeigetragenen Sentimentalität, trotz aller Verzerrungen in der gesellschaftspsychologischen Einstellung und der überziehbaren Werthsmessung soziale Probleme (wie Einstellung und der Sozialist denken kann) eine über literarischer Tasten hinausgehende Kraft zum Erleben des Elementaren kundtun möchte. Mag sie vielfach irrig, weil unerheblich sein, wie in folgendem ner vorragwcine wiedergegebenen Kapitel, so ist dieser Glaube zum Menschen ... und über die Auflösung aller Konflikte hinauszgehen. Und mehr wie etwas, das gerade dem Für-uns-Richtigen vielleicht wesentliche entgegeht.

Der Gaste hielt in Sprechen inne und warf Dara flüchtige Blicke zu. Dann bat er sie plötzlich leise, diese Nacht bei ihr bleiben zu dürfen, wobei er gleichsam schuldbewußt errötete und verwirrt vor ihr stehen blieb. Dara sah erstaunt zu ihm auf. In seinem betretenen Blick war etwas Furchtsam-erwartendes, als ängstige er sich vor ihrer Absage und wünsche sie zugleich.

Dara errötete, erhob sich spöttisch lächelnd und führte Saergei, ihn umarmend, aus dem Zimmer.

'Oeh, geh . . . Du mußt jetzt schlafen. Mach, daß du fortkommst. Das wäre unhygienisch . . .'

Und sie lachte sogar, . . mit einem trockenen, scharfen Lachen. Saergei protestierte nicht weiter, . . murmelte etwas vor sich hin und lachte ebenfalls gezwungen. Aus seinem Benehmen fühlte man etwas wie Dankbarkeit, wie Schuldbewußtsein und etwas Unruhiges, Ungelöstes. An der Schwelle blieb er nochmals stehen und wollte ihr in die Augen sehen, aber sie stieß ihn mit weicher Entschlossenheit hinaus und schloß die Tür.

Gegen zwei Uhr nachts war sie noch immer auf. Ungestüm, mit düster zusammengezogenen Augenbrauen und verließ das Bett, auf der Brust verschränkten Armen ging sie auf und ab, setzte sich zuweilen auf den Diwan, schloß die Augen und warf den Kopf auf die Lehne zurück. Dann zeigte sich auf ihrem, vom Lampenlicht voll erhellten Gesicht brennende Röte und an den unteren Teilen der Wangen und das bebende Eigenleben der erregten Nasenflügel. Und wieder sprang sie auf und ging ruhelos im Zimmer auf und ab.

Auch im Bett konnte sie sich nicht beruhigen, wälzte sich seufzend, hüllte sich bis oben zu und schlug das Decke wieder zurück.

Am Morgen waren ihre Augen mit einem dunklen Müdigkeitsstreifen umrändert, aber im Gesicht lag der Ausdruck einer sonderbar spöttischen, erregten Entschlossenheit.

Oft blickte sie beim Mittagessen über die Gesichter der anderen und lächelte heimlich in sich hinein, um dieses Lächeln sofort wieder zu verstecken. Und etwas Feindseliges folgte diesem Lächeln aufblitzend in ihren Augen, etwas Feindseliges und Unerschütterliches.

Abends zog sie sich ohne jemand ein Wort zu sagen an, nahm das Geld in ihrer Börse und verließ das Haus. Sie lächelte ebenso wie beim Mittagessen, während sie auf der Straße ging.

Sie schlug eine vorher offenbar überlegte Richtung ein, obwohl sie sich öfters umsah und die Häuser aufmerksam betrachtete. In einer kleineren Straße angelangt, wurde ihr Schritt sicherer. An der belebten Kreuzung blieb sie stehen. Zwei Schritte weiter war der Eingang zu einem Hotel. Ueber der Tür brannte eine große Laterne, auf deren Scheiben die Aufschrift zu lesen war „Imperial"; vor der offenen Tür schlummerte friedlich ein livrierter Portier mit einer betressten Mütze.

Dara trat entschlossen zu ihm und fragte laut:

„Haben Sie freie Zimmer?"

Der Portier warf den Kopf hoch, besann sich einen Augenblick schlaftrunken, riß dann die Mütze vom Kopf und antwortete eifrig und mit vielen Verbeugungen:

Das Aktionsbuch
ist erschienen!!

„Bitte, bitte treten Sie ein! . . Hierher, wenn ich bitten darf, wünschen Sie ein großes Zimmer?"

„Das ist gleich. Nur sauber muß es sein."

„Sofort . . ."

Der Portier drückte auf einen Knopf, oben schellte laut eine Glocke, und gleich darauf hörte man weiche, über die Läufer laufende Schritte. Auf dem Treppenabsatz zeigte sich ein Kellner.

„Darf ich Sie bitten, — man wird Ihnen oben zeigen . . ." verbeugte sich der Portier.

Dara stieg langsam und gelassen die wenigen Stufen und folgte dem Kellner an einer langen Reihe von Türen vorbei. Der Mann hatte eine Glatze, die bis zum Halse hinabreichte, ein kleines, spitziges Gesicht, mit versteckten, klugen und durchdringenden Aeuglein darin.

Er stieß eine der Türen auf, zündete die Kerze an und hielt sie in der erhobenen Hand. Das Zimmer war groß, sauber und sogar behaglich.

„Gut. Ich nehme es", sagte Dara.

„Soll das Gepäck vom Bahnhof abgeholt werden?"

„Nein. Ich bin ohne Gepäck."

„Ist eine Teemaschine gefällig?"

„Nein. Ich brauche nichts. Stellen Sie die Kerze auf den Tisch und warten Sie."

Dara nahm vor dem Spiegel stehend den Hut ab, steckte die Nadeln langsam in seinen Filz, legte ihn auf den Tisch, drehte sich zu dem ehrerbietig wartenden Kellner um, und sagte ruhig und befehlend:

„Besorgen Sie mir einen Herrn und führen Sie ihn zu mir ins Zimmer."

Des Kellners Augen wurden größer.

„Sie wünschen? . . ." tragte er behutsam, als fürchte er nicht recht verstanden zu haben.

„Ich wünsche von Ihnen, daß Sie mir einen Herrn herausbringen, Sie führen doch die Männer, die bei Ihnen wohnen, Mädchen zu. Nun, ich verlange von Ihnen, daß Sie mir einen Herrn einführen."

Der Kellner musterte sie mit kurzen Blicken und schien noch immer nichts zu verstehen.

Dara stand stolz und unnahbar vor ihm und runzelte ungeduldig die Brauen.

„Nun, was stehen Sie? Können Sie das?"

„Ganz wie Sie befehlen . . . Nur . . Wünschen Sie das sofort . . ."

„Ja, sofort."

Dem Kellner schien ein Licht aufzugehen.

„Zu Befehl . . . Wie darf ich Sie anmelden?"

„Anna Iwanowna Iwaenko."

„Und der Paß?"

Dara sah ihn aufhaltend an.

„Verfügen Sie sich gefälligst hinaus. Sie sind mir zu gesprächig. Gehen Sie und schicken Sie mir einen anderen."

„Ich bitt' um Verzeihung . . . Ich meinte nur . . . Da wir jeden anmelden müssen . . ."

„Es ist gut. Gehen Sie, und tun Sie, wie ich Ihnen gesagt habe . . ."

„Zu Befehl."

Der Kellner wich rückwärts zur Tür und verschwand. Er mochte das Gefühl gehabt haben, daß die Welt nahe dem Untergang sei.

Dara nahm den Mantel ab, hing ihn auf den Kleiderständer, trat zum Spiegel und ordnete ihr Haar. Die Augen waren glänzend, und um die Wangen spielte leichte Röte. Schwere goldene Flechten krönten die reine, hohe Stirn. Sie lächelte ihrem Spiegelbild zu und begann auf und ab zu gehen.

Es verging ziemlich viel Zeit. Dara ging immer noch mit leicht vorgeneigtem Kopf, mit auf der Brust verschränkten Armen im Zimmer auf und ab.

Als sie des leisen Klopfens an der Tür gewahr wurde, erhob sie den Kopf, sah sich erstaunt um und sagte laut und ruhig:

„Herein!"

Die Tür öffnete sich langsam und ein kleiner Herr schob sich mit kurzen weichen Schrittchen durch den Spalt ins Zimmer. Als sich die Tür, durch die der Glatzkopf und das weiße Vorhemd des Kellners sichtbar wurden, schloß, begann sich der Herr seitwärts und die Hände reibend, als wüsche er sie über der Waschschüssel, zu Dara hinzuschleichen. Die Haare auf der Stirn waren sorgfältig gescheitelt, an seinem Kinn hing ein dichtes, wie aus schwarzer Watte gemachtes Bärtchen, die Augen waren groß und vorstehend und mit lauernder, lüsterner Neugierde auf sie gerichtet.

Daras Blicke überflogen rasch seine Gestalt, ihre Augen verengten sich kühl; sie wartete.

„Guten Tag . . ." sagte er überraschend weich, mit süßlich zärtliche Stimme.

„Guten Tag", antwortete Dara.

Der Herr schlich sich noch näher an sie heran und musterte sie mit einer immer größer werdenden Gier. In den vorstehenden Augen zeigte sich jetzt eine durchaus nicht herrscherische Bewunderung.

„Sie sind erst kurze Zeit hier?"

Daras Blick überflog noch einmal seine ganze Gestalt, dann wandte sie sich plötzlich zur Tür. Der Herr wollte ihr galant zuvorkommen.

„Darf ich für Sie etwas bestellen? . . Wünschen Sie den . . .

. . . Ich will ihm sagen, daß er Sie hinausbegleiten soll. Sie gefallen mir nicht."

Eine Blutwelle schoß dem Herrn ins Gesicht, er warf den Kopf in den Nacken.

„Wie Sie wünschen . . ." sagte er würdevoll und fügte spöttisch lächelnd hinzu: „Nur sind Sie auch nicht ganz so sehr . . . Weil wir doch auch . . . uns mit Dämchen auskennen, so zu sagen . . . . He! . . ."

„Gehen Sie von selbst fort, oder soll ich den Kellner rufen?" Dara blieb an der Glocke stehen.

Mit komisch verletzter Würde seinen Kopf schüttelnd, wandte sich der Herr zur Tür.

„Ganz wie Sie belieben . . ." warf er verächtlich, aber mit leichter Drohung hin. Die Klinke in der Hand, fügte er hinzu: „Ja-a . . . sehr tugendhaft . . . Mein Kompliment."

Und die Tür schloß sich hinter ihm.

Dara mußte unwillkürlich lachen und läutete nach dem Kellner.

In der nächsten Minute stand er vor ihr.

„Hören Sie, mein Lieber," wandte sie sich streng an ihn. „Sie hätten es doch selbst begreifen können, daß ich Greise und Affen nicht brauchen kann. Der Mann muß jung und hübsch sein. Verstehen Sie?"

Der Kellner verbeugte sich ehrfurchtsvoll.

„Vielleicht befehlen Sie einen Studenten?" Er neigte den Kopf treuherzig-schmeichlerisch zur Seite. „Ein Student wohnt hier bei uns, ein ganz junger und sehr . . . passender. Ich hatte gleich an ihn gedacht, er war aber nicht zu Hause. Eben ist er vom Spaziergang zurückgekommen. Er geht jeden Tag spazieren."

„Gut. Führen Sie ihn her."

Der Kellner drehte sich um und glitt geräuschlos aus dem Zimmer.

Dara preßte ihre Hände auf das brennende Gesicht und wurde nachdenklich. Seufzend warf sie einen kurzen Blick auf ihren Hut, befiel ihn eine Weile unentschlossen auf die blitzende Hutnadel und begann hartnäckig den Kopf schüttelnd und wieder mit verschränkten Armen und auf die glänzenden Stiefeln blickte zur Tür.

Man klopfte jetzt ebenso leise und vorsichtig wie vorhin.

„Herein!"

Die Tür öffnete sich unsicher, und auf der Schwelle erschien eine schmächtige, leicht gebeugte Gestalt. Ein junges, verwirrtes Gesicht und schüchterne Augen sahen zu Dara auf.

„Verzeihung . . . Ich glaubte . . . Darf man eintreten?"

Er war sehr verlegen, aber sein Blick wich keinen Augenblick von Dara. Die Tür hinter ihm schloß jemand, der im Korridor gewartet haben mußte.

„Sie dürfen. Kommen Sie nur herein," sagte Dara in einem belehrenden Ton.

Der Student trat einige Schritte näher, blieb stehen und lächelte, wie es Kinder zu tun pflegen, gleichsam schuldbewußt.

147

148

149

DADA

If Expressionism was the first salvo against German art tradition, Dada was the first bloody battle. Convention was quickly unraveling. In Russia, Kasimir Malevich developed Suprematism in 1913 and removed narrative representation from painting. Influenced by another rebellious movement, Futurism, launched by poet F. T. Marinetti in 1909, Dada was in the vanguard of typographic disruption. It was a bridge between art (or anti-art) and the New Typography, which was codified in the mid-1920s. Dada was founded in 1917 at the Caberet Voltaire in Zurich, Switzerland, by expatriate artists and writers who had deserted their respective homelands to protest war and the society that promoted it. Dada was a uprising against a world that was capable of unspeakable horrors. Its rejection of bourgeois art (and conventional typography) was an attack on both abhorrent social and cultural values and the artistic styles and mannerisms that symbolized these values. Dada spread from Zurich to Cologne, Berlin, and New York. Among the common visual methods of public address, Dadaists used periodicals with titles such as *Dada*, *Revolution*, and *Neue Jugend* to critically expound on diverse social and political themes. In demolishing pretense, Dada was an enemy of bourgeois taste.

---

146. NEUE JUGEND, *periodical page, 1917. Designer: John Heartfield.*

147. NEUE JUGEND, *periodical page, 1917. Designer: John Heartfield.*

148. REVOLUTION, *periodical cover, 1918. Designer unknown.*

149. DADA ZURICH, *catalog cover, 1920. Designer unknown.*

DADA

Consistent with the Dadaists preference for photography and photomontage, which they deemed were original expressions of an industrial society, over the more antiquated brush and paint on canvas, publication layouts eschewed conventional formats and established hierarchies of headlines and subheads. Columns of justified and ragged type often were skewed beyond conventional margins; multiple type weights and faces from different type families were used unharmoniously in a single composition; and hot-metal type material (heavy rules and stock illustrations) were strewn willy nilly throughout the pages. A typical Dada design looked, in printer's terms, like the contents of a hellbox (a receptacle for smashed and broken type bodies). This willful typographic anarchy reflected the chaos in the wake of the Great War, but more importantly, it marked the battle lines against archaic tradition and bourgeois mediocrity. Dadaism saw itself as a provocation against the cozy values and words printed on handmade paper and bound in gilt-edged pig-skin. They cut up newspapers and juggled the words around to form collages. "But juggling letters does not on its own constitute typography," wrote typographer Otl Aicher. "It is meaningful in itself, but it tends to run counter to typography's objective of transmitting meaning." Words were set to create moods, simulate sound, and summon virtual pictures of the ideas presented. Although Dadaists did not design type fonts a typographic code developed that signaled a revolutionary spirit in graphic design.

150

150. DER DADA, *periodical cover, 1919. Designer: Raoul Hausmann.*

151. DADA-MESSE, *exhibition poster, 1919. Designer: Raoul Hausmann.*

152. DER DADA, *periodical cover, 1919. Designer: Raoul Hausmann.*

153. MOUVEMENT DADA, *periodical cover, c. 1919. Designer unknown.*

154. MECANO, *periodical cover, 1922. Designer: Theo van Doesburg.*

KUNSTHANDLUNG DR. OTTO BURCHARD
BERLIN, LÜTZOW-UFER 13

Geöffnet täglich von 10—1 Uhr vormittags
und 3—6½ Uhr nachmittags

Eintritt 3 Mk.

Die Bewegung Dada führt zur Aufhebung des Kunsthandels

ERSTE INTERNATIONALE
DADA-MESSE

Veranstaltet von
Marschall G. Grosz,
Dadasoph Raoul Hausmann,
Monteurdada John Heartfield

Katalog / Preis 1,70 Mk.

Ausstellung und Verkauf dadaistischer Erzeugnisse

Der dadaistische Mensch ist der radikale Gegner der Ausbeutung, der Sinn der Ausbeutung schafft nur der Dumme und der dadaistische Mensch haßt die Dummheit und liebt den Unsinn! Also zeigt sich der dadaistische Mensch als wahrhaft real gegenüber der stinkenden Verlogenheit des in seinem Lehnstuhl verreckenden Familienvaters und Kapitalisten. R. Hausmann.

151

152

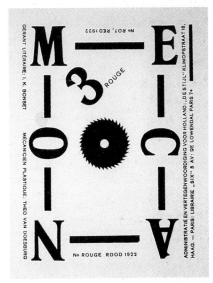

154

HET

Nᴿ 14

OVERZICHT

D
ECEMBER

1922

AVANT-GARDE MODERN

After World War I, paradigm shifts in the form and function of art, architecture, and even photography from bourgeois indulgence to experimental media broke the strictures imposed by academics and increased the range of art's influence over everyday life. Advocacy of "the whole work of art" challenged the inequality between fine and applied art. Modernism, which comprised kindred yet independent groups of European cultural movements and schools, proffered the seamless marriage of art and design as integral to the betterment of humankind. A utopian view held that art was not an entertainment for the elite, but a utilitarian product for the masses. The artist's touch enhanced all aspects of life, especially graphic design and advertising, which had been constricted by archaic rules and tech-

a symbol and tool of transforma- tors of the "new spirit." Early F. T. Marinetti produced the first he called "words in freedom." From wrote and designed the first con- nology. Type, which became both tion, was one of the first indica- experiments began in 1909 when of many typographic manifestos 1913 to 1916, Guillaume Apollinaire crete poems, titled *Calligrames.* These inspired a reevaluation of typography that emerged in Russia, Germany, Holland, Italy, and Eastern Europe and rejected ornamentalism. Codified by Jan Tschichold under the rubric "Elementary Typography" in 1925 and dubbed "The New Typography" in 1928, this replaced ancient verities and timeworn alphabets with asymmetrical layouts, sans serif typefaces, and the commingling of type and photomontage (typofoto). Rooted in the turmoils of the new century, the rationale for the New Typography was legibility and readability. Considering central-axis compositions to be lackluster, New Typography sought to "project a persuasive message into the reader's psyche with the highest immediacy of meaning...," as L. Sandusky wrote in *PM* magazine in 1938. The tools included type in asymmetrical relationships or masses, lines, arrows, bullets of color, and oblique and vertical direction contrasts. Unlike past typographic practice, avant-garde Modern type arrangement was influenced by abstract painting.

OPPOSITE: HET OVERZICHT, *periodical cover (Antwerp), 1922. Designer: Jazef Peeters.*
ABOVE: CZEKOLADA PLUTOS, *catalog cover (Poland), 1925. Designer: Henryk Berlewi.*

FUTURISM
ITALY

In 1905, F. T. Marinetti laid the foundation for an activist art movement that heralded poetic free verse in a radical departure from the conventions of poetry. His goal was to affirm individual liberty against social hierarchies and to celebrate intuition as the key to creative expression. In free verse (*parole in libertá*) he found an ideological model, and in 1909 he published the first Futurist manifesto, which announced that "the Futurist writer will make use of free verse, an orchestration of images and sounds in motion," to express contemporary life "intensified by the speeds made possible by steam and electricity, on land, on the seas, and in the air." The Futurist movement did not forsake painting; rather, its artists revered speed in their kineticist canvases and typographic compositions. Like later Dada periodicals, early Futurist manifestoes and onomatopoetic poems employed type to simulate the sounds of machines that heroicized the aesthetics of speed. The Futurist revolution "reinvented" every aspect of life, including advertising, books, and clothing. Advertising was the perfect medium for expressing Futurist ideals, and the "Futurist style," as codified by Fortunato Depero, was applied to commercial products. The book-object—with dislocated letters floating on pages and experimental covers made from metal and bound with metal bolts—was a rejection of traditional bourgeois standards. The Futurists also advocated the creation of dazzling, colored phosphorescent clothes that made the street into a theater of the absurd.

155

155. DEPERO, *exhibition announcement, 1929. Designer: Fortunato Depero.*

156. DINAMO FUTURISTA, *periodical cover, 1926. Designer: Fortunato Depero.*

157. CORDIAL CAMPARI, *advertisement, 1933. Designer: Fortunato Depero.*

158. DUCE! DUCE! DUCE!, *editorial layout, c. 1930. Designer unknown.*

159. SAVOOOIAAAA, *poetry postcard, 1917. F. T. Marinetti.*

160. NEW YORK, *postcard, 1929. Designer: Fortunato Depero.*

156

157

158

159

160

161

162

163

164

MILANO 20 FEBBRAIO 1929 - VII - c. c. postale - quindicinale illustrato

9   3 lire

SECOLO XX

XX

F. Depero
Rovereto

In questo numero:
DIEGO ANGELI
GIUSEPPE BEVIONE
LUIGI CHIARELLI
CRISPOLTO CRISPOLTI
LUCIO D'AMBRA
CARLO LINATI
ADRIANO LUALDI
FILIPPO MEDA
L. A. MONDINI
PIETRO STOPPANI
ERNESTO VERCESI
NICOLA ZINGARELLI
Una musica di
NINO CATTOZZO

QUARANTA PAGINE
DEDICATE ALL'EVENTO
DELLA CONCILIAZIONE

165

161-162. FUTURISMO, *periodical cover,*
1933–1932. Designer unknown.

163. ITALIANE, *exhibition*
announcement, 1930. Designer unknown.

164. IL LIBRO..., *prospectus, 1930.*
Designer unknown.

165. SECOLO XX, *periodical cover, 1929.*
Designer: Fortunato Depero.

FUTURISM
ITALY

Benito Mussolini announced, "It is Marinetti who instilled in me the feeling of the ocean and the power of the machine." Indeed Futurism and Fascism were initially joined in their contempt for the bourgeoisie. The Fascists, who also embraced the trappings of ancient Rome, used the Futurist avant-garde as a tool for exciting youth, although eventually they barely tolerated the eccentricities of Futurism. Before turning entirely to social realism, which personified the individual subsumed by the state, Futurism inspired the official Fascist style of commercial art common on both propaganda posters and in commercial advertisements during the first decade of the regime. Kinetic-looking, often mechanically drawn typefaces, sometimes shaded and usually with pointed ascenders and descenders, gave the illusion of speed. The original Futurist *parole in libertá* purposefully used existing roman typefaces in unconventional ways to underscore the Futurists' fervent repudiation of tradition. Later styles of display faces were almost parodies of what a Futurist type should look like. Depero was the master of commercial futurist lettering, using a curious synthesis of avant-garde, sans serif alphabets and roman-letter stone inscriptions. Futurist lettering ran the gamut from comparatively restrained to outlandishly gaudy. In the 1930s, when Fascism became more entrenched and intolerant of avant-garde experiments, Futurism dissipated as a dynamic fine and applied art movement.

CONSTRUCTIVISM
RUSSIA

In 1913, Kasimir Malevich invented Suprematism, nonobjective art characterized by the symbolic juxtaposition of squares and rectangles framed by negative space. Under his influence younger artists took the abstraction further into the province of commercial art. In 1915, Vladimir Tatlin experimented with what he called a "machine art" or "product art," collages and montages constructed from industrial products. His approach, known as Constructivism, had various progenitors, including Alexander Rodchenko and Vladimir Mayakowsky, who designed collage covers for the journal *LEF*, the cultural gazette of Constructivism, and Lazar (El) Lissitzky, who combined Suprematist and Constructivist elements into experimental designs that he called "Prouns." After the Bolshevik Revolution, many of these avant-garde artists applied their experiments to utilitarian graphic design for products and commodities; they called this "Productivist Art." Lissitzky's compositions were Suprematist melanges of geometric shapes that symbolized Bolshevism's triumph over the reactionaries; underlying his radical form-making was a political and social agenda. Constructivism and Productivism were taught at the Vkhutemas Higher Artistic Technical Studios—a new art for a new age—and quickly evolved into a typographic style that imbued the printed page with dynamism and encouraged an illiterate population to take notice.

166. FOR THE VOICE, *book of poems, 1923. Designer: El Lissitzky.*

167. DEATH RAY, *poster, 1926. Designer unknown.*

166

167

168

169

170

171

168. WHAT DID YOU DO FOR THE
FRONT, *poster, 1920. Designer:*
El Lissitzky.

169. THE ART OF THE OCTOBER
REVOLUTION, *book cover, c. 1925.*
Designer unknown.

170. LAQUERED TIGHTS, *book cover,*
c. 1925. Designer: A. Kruchenykh.

171. YOUNG BRIGADE, *book cover,*
c. 1925. Designer: Solomon Telengater.

CONSTRUCTIVISM RUSSIA

The Russian avant-garde developed a vocabulary of typographic discordance that was born out of necessity yet became an expression of the revolutionary times. After the Russian involvement in the First World War came to a precipitous halt, the nation was plagued by shortages. Printing materials—paper, type, ink—were at a premium, and yet printing was the primary means of communicating with the populace. Constructivist typography developed its distinctive look—letters and words at right angles framed by bold rules and borders printed in one or two primary colors—in part because the limited typecase materials prevented all but such reductive approaches. Moreover, garish ornamentation was associated with Czarist and oligarchic indulgences. The avant-garde artist/designers also looked to Holland and Germany for inspiration, and through the publications that promoted the Modern avant-garde they found kindred sensibilities in Dada, Neoplacticism, Futurism, Cubism, and other isms. The Russian typographer Solomon Telengater, for one, stressed the dynamics of functional typography and what he called the "cinematographicity" of concurrent pages. The cross-pollination of different European designers and the sharing of their typographical conceits gave rise to the New Typography.

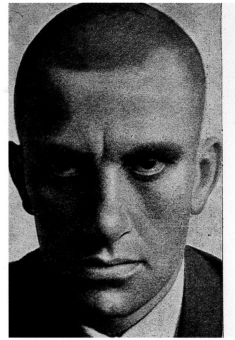

172

173

172. IN FULL VOICE, *book title page, c. 1932. Designer: Solomon Telengater.*

173. THE WORD BELONGS TO KIRSANOV, *poem, 1930. Designer: Solomon Telengater.*

174. PA, *periodical cover, 1931. Designer: Solomon Telengater.*

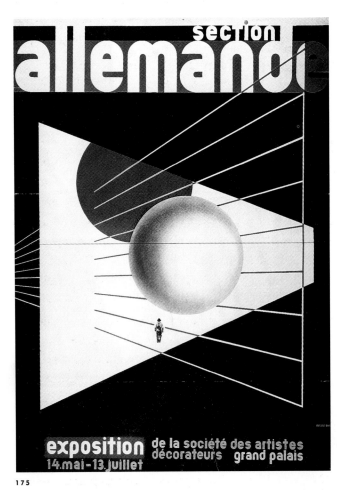

175. SECTION ALLEMANDE, *exhibition poster, 1930. Designer: Herbert Bayer.*

176. PHOEBUS-PALAST, *movie poster, 1926. Designer: Jan Tschichold.*

177-178. USSR, *catalog pages, 1928. Designer: El Lissitzky.*

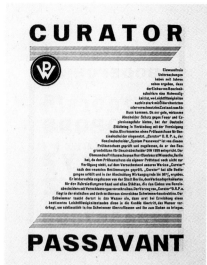

179   180

181

182

THE NEW TYPOGRAPHY GERMANY

The Bauhaus, the center of Modernist design pedagogy in Western Europe, was preceded by the Weimar *Kunstgewerbeschule*, a state-sponsored school that taught applied arts in the *Jugendstil* style. In 1915, architect Walter Gropius became director, and beginning after World War I the curriculum included typography and graphic design. In accordance with its state charter, in 1923 the Bauhaus mounted its first major exhibition, *Staatliches Bauhaus in Weimar 1919–1923*, which revealed the seismic shift from traditional typography to Constructivism in both books and advertising. The addition a few years earlier of Hungarian Constructivist Laszlo Moholy-Nagy to the Bauhaus faculty and the creation of a preliminary typography course had ushered in the experimental phase of Bauhaus typography, notable for its marriage of type and photography. For the Bauhaus catalog, in an essay titled "The New Typography," Moholy-Nagy stressed that "typography is an instrument of communication. It must present precise information in a suggestive form . . . For legibility, the message must never suffer from *a priori* aesthetics. The letter types must never be forced into a pre-planned form. . . ." The need for new functionality introduced designers to the concept of *elementare typografie*, dynamic compositions using minimal means, which underlies what in 1928 Jan Tschichold codified as *Die Neue Typographie* (The New Typography), the unprecedented synthesis of Constructivist, Bauhaus, and de Stijl design concepts.

183

184

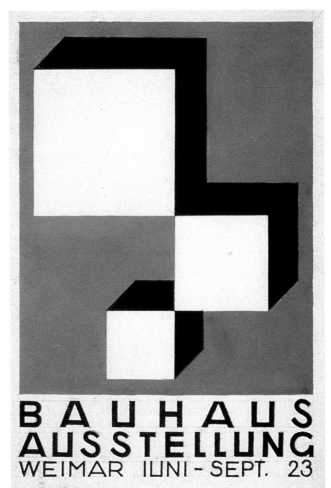

185

186

187

GESTALTUNG DER REKLAME

Die Reklame ist die Handschrift des Unternehmers! Wie die Handschrift ihren Urheber, so verrät die Reklame Art, Kraft und Fähigkeit einer Unternehmung.

Das Maß der Leistungsfähigkeit, Qualitätspflege, Solidität, Energie und Großzügigkeit eines Unternehmens spiegelt sich in Sachlichkeit, Klarheit, Form und Umfang seiner Reklame.

Hochwertige Qualität der Ware erste Bedingung des Erfolges! Die zweite: Geeignete Absatzorganisation; deren unentbehrlicher Faktor ist gute Reklame!

■ DIE GUTE REKLAME

ist sachlich	1
ist klar und knapp	2
sie verwendet moderne Mittel	3
hat Schlagkraft der Form	4
ist billig.	5

1

Die gute Reklame ist sachlich. Sie macht nur Aussagen, die der Wahrheit entsprechen. Vertrauen muß erobert und bewahrt werden. Die Reklame darf nicht Erwartungen erwecken, denen nicht Tatsachen entsprechen. Gute Reklame verdeutlicht eindringlich und eindeutig die guten und die besonderen Eigenschaften des Angebots.

2

Die gute Reklame ist klar und knapp. Der moderne Mensch geizt mit der Zeit. Wer liest langen Text bei Hunderten von Anzeigen und Plakaten, wer hört auf lange Reden? Wenig zeigen! Wenig sagen! Das Wenige oft! Steter Schlag in selbe Kerbe haut durch. Die gute Reklame nimmt Rücksicht auf die Zeit des Publikums, vertraut der eigenen Zähligkeit, ist vornehm, verzichtet auf Geschwätz. Schrift sei lesbar, deutlich, die Formulierung klar, bei größter Knappheit unmißverständlich! Rätselhaftigkeit (sparsam verwandt) kann Reiz sein zu stärkerem Interesse. Die Lösung muß um so prägnanter sein. Auch in der Darstellung beschränkt sich gute Reklame auf das Notwendige, stellt immer das Wesentliche, und nur das Wesentliche, auffallend, deutlich herausspringend hin.

188

80

THE NEW TYPOGRAPHY
GERMANY

The Bauhaus was the mecca for progressive designers, including Russian Constructivist El Lissitzky and Dutch de Stijl founder Theo van Doesburg. In addition, exemplars of modern type and advertising also emerged from the student body. Joost Schmidt, who designed the first Bauhaus exhibition poster in a Constructivist style, taught and applied his experiments to work for freelance clients such as YKO, a leading producer of office supplies. It was businesses like these, patrons of progressive design, that helped foster acceptance for the new typographic approaches throughout Germany. As a student in 1923, Herbert Bayer designed ersatz money for the inflation-ridden treasury of Thurginia, and after the Bauhaus moved to Dessau in 1924, he taught in the printing department. His typography was based on the combination of simple optical forms—geometric shapes, diagonal rules, primary colors—which became a trademark for the Bauhaus. Writing in a 1928 issue of the Bauhaus magazine, Bayer stated, "Elementary typography . . . has without a doubt, showed us the way towards new basic typographic work. It proposed making full use of the various materials already available and developing a technique of setting type in new forms." Among these new forms, Bayer designed a lowercase alphabet called "universal." In a 1939 issue of *PM* magazine, he wrote, "Every period has its own formal and cultural features, expressed in its contemporary habits of life, in its architecture and literature. The same applies to language and writing."

189

190

183-185. BAUHAUS PRINTING, *posters and postcards, c. 1925–28. Designer: Herbert Bayer.*

186. YKO, *advertisement, 1924. Designer: Joost Schmidt.*

187. UHER TYPE, *advertisement, 1932. Designer: Joost Schmidt.*

188. DIE GUTE REKLAME, *advertising guidelines, 1924. Designer: Max Burchartz.*

189. STAATLICHES BAUHAUS IN WEIMAR 1919–1923, *catalog cover, 1923. Designer: Herbert Bayer.*

190. UNIVERSAL, *alphabet, 1925. Type designer: Herbert Bayer.*

THE NEW TYPOGRAPHY
GERMANY

The New Typography was featured in a 1925 issue of *Typographische Mitteilungen,* a Leipzig-based trade journal whose readers were professional printers and typographers. Guest edited by Jan Tschichold, a young typographer from Cologne, the magazine encouraged printers to emulate the functional, elemental, and dynamic design philosophies of the avant-garde. Printers were introduced to methods which, though unorthodox at that time, were soon adopted by business. Some of the designers belonged to a group of progressives known as the *Ring Neuer Webegestalter* (circle of new advertising designers), which championed the New Typography as an alternative to the mediocrity that prevailed. Individually, some designers, including Max Burchartz's "Werbebau" in Bochum, Walter Dexel's studio in Jena, and Kurt Schwitters's *Merz* in Hannover, established their own commercial advertising studios that wed art to utility. *Merz* was the non-sense name of Schwitters's Dada periodical in which he published articles, manifestoes, and experiments and collaborated with other artist/designers. They examined how far dynamic tension between type, white space, and primary color could be pushed. In *Merz* 11 (1925), Schwitters reproduced a selection of advertisements, influenced by Lissitzky, for Pelikan inks using only red and black and bold type. Schwitters and van Doesburg also tested the limits of children's book illustration in *Die Scheuche* (The Scarecrow) using letters and typecase materials to tell the story.

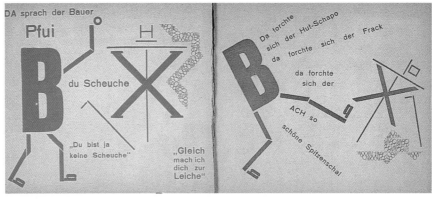

191

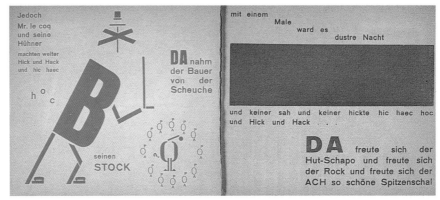

192

193

191-193. DIE SCHEUCHE (THE SCARE-CROW), *children's book, 1925. Designers: Kurt Schwitters and Theo van Doesburg.*

194-195. MERZ 8/9, *periodical cover and page, 1924. Designers: Kurt Schwitters and Theo van Doesburg.*

196-198. MERZ 11, *periodical cover and pages, 1924. Designer: Kurt Schwitters.*

194

196

195

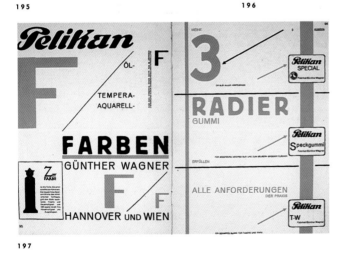

197

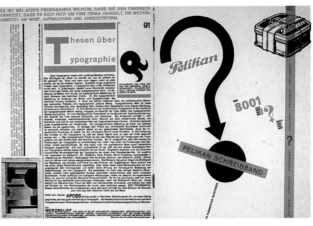

198

199

200

201

202

![tank no. 1½ ljubljana, s.h.s. lioubliana, s.c.s.]

203

204

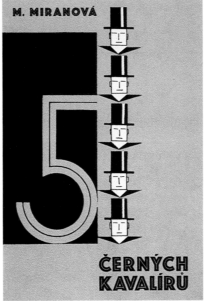

205

THE NEW TYPOGRAPHY
EASTERN EUROPE

In Poland, Hungary, Yugoslavia, and Czechoslovakia, the New Typography was practiced by designers who were either schooled at or influenced by the Bauhaus or Vkhutemas. But Constructivism was not simply an import. Warsaw and Cracow had healthy design communities and published experimental journals such as *Blok*, *Praeasens*, and *Dzwignia*. Henryk Berlewi, of Warsaw, developed *mechano-faktura* constructions, ran his own Reklama Mechano advertising agency, and pushed the boundaries of Polish design. Prague was a veritable Bauhaus annex; Devitstil, the progressive Czech art movement, was as concerned with promoting abstract art and functional graphics. The marriage of the two could be found in the typofoto of Ladislav Sutnar and the Constructivist typography of Karel Teige, who designed the journal *Red*. Budapest had a progressive Modern type culture promoted through the art magazine *MA* and the trade journal *Magyar Grafika*. And in the city of Ljubljana, Yugoslavia, Modern type was championed through the journal *Tank*.

199. A KERÉK, *periodical cover, 1930. Designer unknown.*

200. MENTOR CAMERAS, *advertisement, c. 1933. Designer: J. Pécsi.*

201. ZIJEME 1931, *periodical cover, 1931. Designer: Ladislav Sutnar.*

202. SZENZÁCIÓK, *advertisement, 1928. Designer unknown.*

203. TANK, *periodical cover, 1927. Editor: Josip Pavlcek.*

204. MASSAG, *advertisement, c. 1930. Designer unknown.*

205. CERNYCH KAVALIRU, *book cover, 1930. Designer: V. Kastner.*

THE NEW TYPOGRAPHY
EASTERN EUROPE

Progressive graphic design flourished in the Eastern European capitals. In Budapest, Alexander Bortnyik founded the Mühely workshop, a private school for commercial art. Similar schools and workshops elsewhere promoted the New Typography as method and philosophy. Students were exposed to its application through exhibitions and trade journals that featured indigenous work as well as that imported from Holland, Russia, and Germany. One well-circulated and influential commentary on the subject was published by typographer Walter Dexel in 1927 in the *Frankfurter Zeitung*. This article (ironically typeset in Fraktur) expressed the principles that exemplified Modern practice. "The goal of the new typography is an objective and impersonal presentation, free of individuality," he wrote. "Our highest aim is legibility and our best type is the one which everybody can decipher quickly. If writing exclusively in lowercase letters becomes familiar usage, we shall use it, because we realize its economy." But despite the declarations, Dexel also insisted that "one can hardly make recipes and we should guard against all dogmas, even the factually correct ones. . . . It is not essential that a printed communication be read from first word to last in consecutive order. . . ." Messages, he said, must appeal to the audience's different interests. It is this notion of custom accessibility that distinguished the new typography from the old. This was also the essence of a new approach to advertising that sought to serve rather than simply shout at the public.

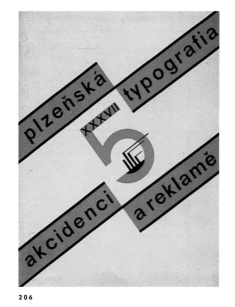

206

207

208

206. TYPOGRAFIA, *periodical cover, 1930.*

207. MAGYAR GRAFIKA, *periodical cover, 1931. Designer: Tadée Gronowski.*

208. REKLAMA MECHANO, *prospectus cover, 1924. Designer: Henryk Berlewi.*

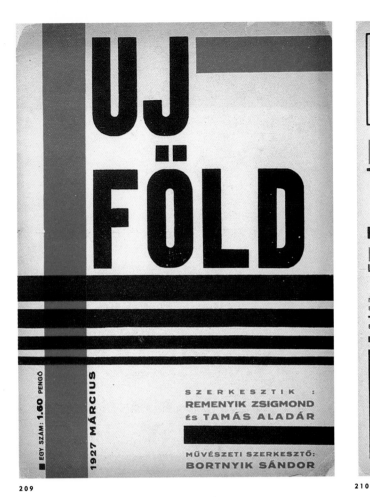

209

210

211

212

213

214

209-210. UJ FÖLD, *periodical cover and advertising page, 1927. Designer: Bortnyik Sandor.*

211. RED, *periodical cover, 1928. Designer: Karel Teige.*

212-213. DOKUMENTUM, *periodical covers, 1932. Designer: Lajoss Kasack.*

214. ECCE HOMO, *poetry, 1923. Designer: Hercz Gyórgy.*

215

216

217

215. N K F , *advertisement, 1926. Designer:*
Piet Zwart.

216. DE GEMEENSCHAP, *periodical cover,*
1930. Designer: Paul Schuitema.

217. WENDINGEN, *magazine cover, 1929.*
Designer: Vilmos Huszar.

218

219

DE STIJL
THE NETHERLANDS

In Holland it is said, "God made the World, the Dutch made Holland." This because the Dutch landscape is almost entirely man-made, reclaimed from the sea and fortified by a system of dykes. It is in this orderly landscape, where right angles and straight lines define the topography, that an avant-garde design movement that treats such geometry as a sacrament was born. In 1917, Theo van Doesburg (born Christian E. M. Küpper), Vilmos Huszar, Antony Kok, Bart van der Leck, Piet Mondrian, and J. J. P. Oud founded the group they called de Stijl (the style). Van Doesburg originally wanted to call the group's journal *The Straight Line*, but instead agreed to *De Stijl*. Rectilinearity was common to all Modern movements, but for the Dutch it was a matter of faith. In fact, the rigidity that defined de Stijl was the direct result of its members' Calvinist background. In addition to the rectangle, the key elements of de Stijl painting and design were the use of black, white, grey, and the primaries red, blue, and yellow. Mondrian demanded strict adherence, but van Doesburg introduced oblique rectangles and the color green as contributing to more dynamic compositions. According to Mondrian, this deviation from the fundamental principles destroyed the essential objectives of the movement. Mondrian disassociated himself in 1925. By then, van Doesburg had lost interest in such strict rules and his faith in de Stijl.

218. DUPLEX KABEL, *advertisement, c. 1924. Designer: Piet Zwart.*

219. OPBOUW, *periodical cover, 1935. Designer: Paul Schuitema.*

DE STIJL
THE NETHERLANDS

Like Dada, de Stijl was an anti-art art movement. In a 1926 manifesto published in *De Stijl* titled "The End of Art," Theo van Doesburg declared that "Art, whose function nobody knows, hinders the function of life. For the sake of progress we must destroy Art." Ironically, the results of his rebellion against art are considered exemplary artifacts of the Modern period today. In his crusade against outmoded and failed ideas, van Doesburg became a vociferous advocate of a total union of fine and applied arts, and he thus brought type design and typography into de Stijl since it was consistent with the idea of straight lines and rectilinear geometry. Although his radicalism made Bauhaus administrators suspicious and they did not invite him to teach at the school, van Doesburg conducted private classes on his own in Weimar for Bauhaus students, who studied de Stijl painting and typography. Back in the Netherlands, Piet Zwart, an architect and industrial designer, was influenced by van Doesburg and de Stijl principles, which he applied to his commercial typography for industrial and corporate clients. Zwart used Gothic and Egyptian type in bold asymmetric compositions that relied on the size and juxtaposition of letters to convey both literal and symbolic messages. One of Zwart's most inventive colleagues was Paul Schuitema, who mastered typofoto for his commercial clients, likewise using bold sans serif faces where the scale of the words in relation to each other gave each advertisement its dynamism and eye-catching appeal.

220

221

222

223

220. TEKA 546, *brochure cover, 1938. Designer: Henry Cahn.*

221. COPPER WIRE—ANY SHAPE, *advertisement, 1924. Designer: Piet Zwart.*

222. UITNOODIGING, *advertisement, c. 1934. Designer unknown.*

223. PAPER: INSULATED, *advertisement, c. 1925. Designer: Piet Zwart.*

224. DRUKKERIJ TRIO, *catalog page, 1931. Designer: Piet Zwart.*

een kleine keuze uit onze lettercollectie

27

THE NEW TYPOGRAPHY ENGLAND

England did not give birth to the European Modern typographic movement, but it did have a viable avant-garde that spawned progressive typography. Vorticism, lead by Wyndham Lewis, was the British version of Italian Futurism. Taking its name from the centrifugal force of kinetic power, the Vorticists painted canvases that celebrated the twentieth century, the machine age, speed, and war. Its appropriately titled journals, *Blast* and *Enemy*, typographically influenced by Marinetti's *parole in liberta*, employed bold gothic letters set in asymmetric compositions to underscore and give voice to the movement's unorthodox declarations on art, culture, and life. These avant-gardisms did not give rise to new type designs, but influenced typographers who sought alternatives from traditional English design (and from *ye olde English* pastiche). While the foremost Modern faces were designed in Germany, England was the birthplace of two important sans serif typefaces: Eric Gill's Gill Sans and Edward Johnston's alphabet commissioned for the London Underground. These faces were frequently used by both progressive designers and commercial printers. English Modernism was the basis for the contemporary typography that emerged in the abstract posters and book jackets of E. McKnight Kauffer and other modernists who were active during the late 1920s and 1930s.

225. THE ENEMY, *periodical cover, 1927. Designer: Wyndham Lewis.*

226-228. GILL SANS (EXTRA HEAVY, CAMEO, ULTRA BOLD), *alphabets, 1927–1930. Type designer: Eric Gill.*

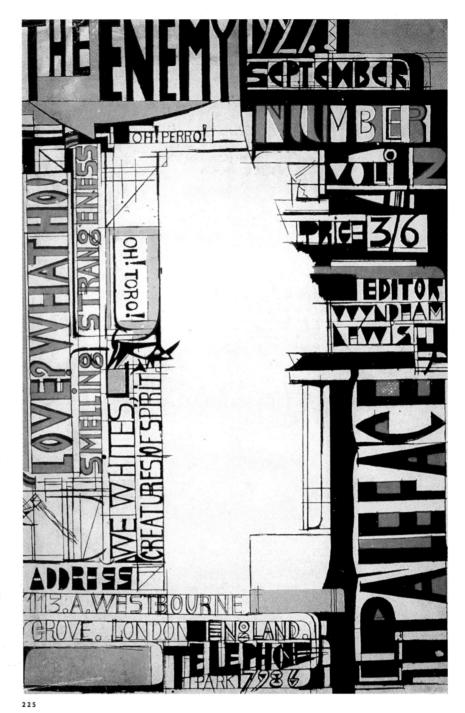

225

MODERN Com
226

MODERN COM
227

Modern Comm
228

229

230

231

232

229. SHELL, *poster, 1929. Designer: E. McKnight Kauffer.*

230. THE MYSTERIOUS UNIVERSE, *book jacket, 1929. Designer unknown.*

231. SHAKEN BY THE WIND, *book jacket, c. 1930. Designer: E. McKnight Kauffer.*

232. QUACK QUACK, *book jacket, 1936. Designer: E. McKnight Kauffer.*

JAN.1932

DEWITT CLINTON H.S.

MOSHOLU PKWAY

NEW YORK CITY

A.MORTIMER CLARK

PRINCIPAL

COMMERCIAL MODERN

In the 1920s, modernism with a small *m* (also known as moderne, modernistic, and art deco) was the bourgeois compromise between traditional and radical design. Introduced in France in 1925 at the *Exposition internationale des arts décoratifs et industriels modernes* and spread throughout Europe and Asia, what later came to be known as the deco style made its way to the United States, where it was harnessed as an advertising tool to give the veneer of progress to products. In a 1933 article titled "The Dividends of Beauty" in *Advertising Arts*, Earnest Elmo Calkins wrote, "Modernism offered the opportunity of expressing the inexpressible, of suggesting not so much a motor car as speed, not so much a gown as style, not so much a compact as beauty."

Avant-Garde Modernism sparked the mannerism, but its only similarities with commercial modernism were superficial characteristics. Otherwise, moderne was a marriage of modernistic art and contemporary merchandising. There was nothing utopian about the need to move goods off the shelves, and if modernistic type and

other contemporary graphic effects did the job, then so be it. "The New Typography was a philosophy not a style," critiqued L. Sandusky in *PM* magazine. "It was largely the failure to understand this which produced around 1928 . . . the 'Dark Cloud Era' and retarded in America an international movement." However, the idea that the public would wholeheartedly embrace the avant-garde was naive. History proves that cultural vanguards appeal to a very savvy few, and the austerity of avant-garde design was difficult to accept in its purist form. Nevertheless, since the New Typography was intended to reform the existing media, it was destined to be adulterated. Every nation with a consumer economy subscribed to modernity, each in its unique way. Type was a major component of this trend, and the late 1920s and 1930s was the time when type design accelerated to meet the immense needs of advertising. Like other mass consumables, typefaces were promoted through specimen sheets as fashion accessories.

OPPOSITE: DEWITT CLINTON HIGH SCHOOL, *high school yearbook cover, 1932. Designer unknown.*
ABOVE: LA LETTRE ARTISTIQUE & MODERNE, *type specimen book, 1934. Designer unknown.*

FRANCE

Art Moderne, the commercial phase of Modernism, was born in France prior to World War I, but its development was interrupted by the war. The concerted marketing of the style, therefore, begins in 1925 at what was the playground of modernity in Paris along the banks of the Seine. The *Exposition internationale des arts décoratifs et industriels modernes* was a grand showroom for modernistic wares produced by or for the world's leading furniture, clothes, cosmetic, and sundry manufacturers. Although the Soviet Union was represented by an imposing Constructivist pavilion and Le Courbusier displayed his *Esprit Nouveau* architecture in a likewise historically important structure, the Exposition was dominated by commercial design and exhibited all its various trappings. Type design was tied to what was called the "window dressing" aesthetics of the day, with foundries producing scores of display, novelty, and froufrou faces to meet the demands of a growing advertising industry. Deberny & Peignot was the most prolific and sophisticated foundry for both traditionally elegant type and the exhibitionist novelties that were on the fashion-curve. Style books were also published to encourage the adoption of the style. *Mise en Page,* by typographer A. Tolmer, was the most inclusive in instructing advertising designers in the proper care and use of type in modernistic compositions.

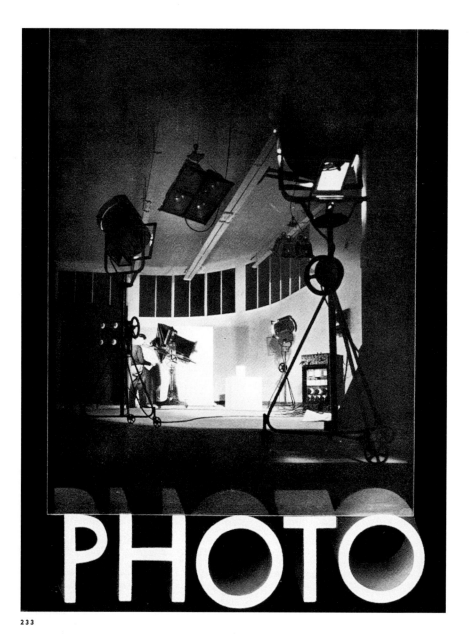

233. PHOTO, *type specimen (Deberny & Peignot), 1930. Type designer unknown.*

234. EUROPE, *type specimen (Deberny & Peignot), c. 1930. Type designer: Paul Renner.*

235

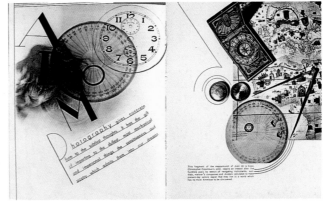

236

237

238

239

235-239. MISE EN PAGE (ENGLISH
EDITION), *book cover and interior pages,*
1932. Designer: A. Tolmer.

FRANCE

France built its economy on commercial Modernism. In contrast to Art Nouveau, which had an impact on the Parisian cityscape but failed to achieve widespread public acceptance, moderne design was ubiquitous in all forms, from buildings to matchboxes. After the ostentatious artifice that preceded it, the straight line became the paradigm of beauty. Yet early Moderne ornament included an array of flowers, animals, and nymphs integrated into geometric patterns comprised of zigzags, chevrons, and lightning bolts. Designers playfully borrowed Ancient Egyptian, Mayan, and Oriental motifs. In a nation that suffered the ravages of war, Moderne design signified a return to prewar prosperity. Business was quick to accept any tool that stimulated consumption, so advertising agencies, poster ateliers, and type shops grew. The poster was the testing ground for new lettering, and various foundries began to design, copy, and pirate original alphabets. Before the war, Fonderies Deberny & Peignot marketed the most popular original typefaces in France, among them Nicolas Cochin, Moreau le Jeune, and Le Naudin. In the 1930s A. M. Cassandre added to this inventory when he designed Bifur, a unique display face that A. Tolmer called the "phenomena of advertising," and Peignot (in honor of Charles Peignot), which remains the quintessential Moderne typeface.

240. PEIGNOT, *type specimen, 1937. Type designer: A. M. Cassandre.*

241. BIFUR, *type specimen, 1929. Type designer: A. M. Cassandre.*

242-243. NOVELTY FACES, *type specimens, c. 1933. Type designer unknown.*

ABCDEFGHIi

JKLMNOPQR

STUVWXYZ

242

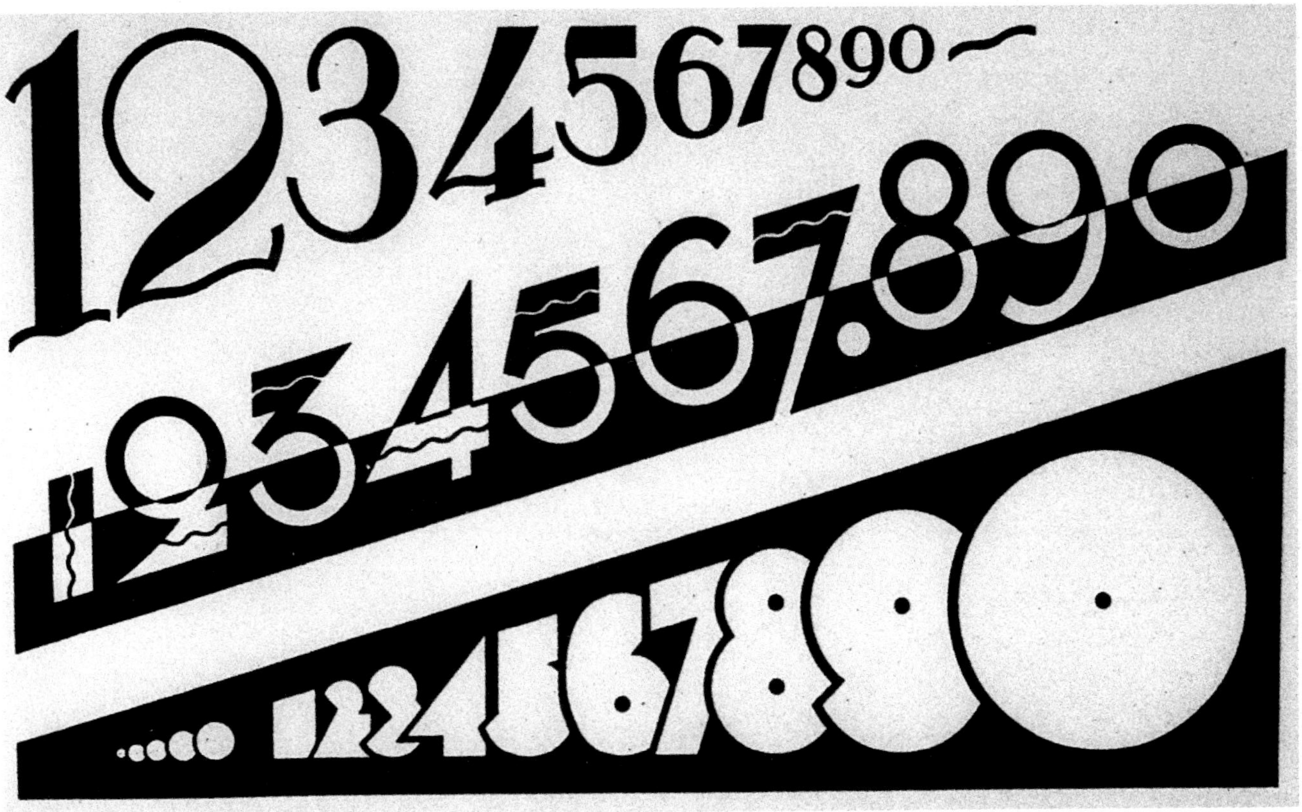

1234567890~

1234567890

1234567890

243

99

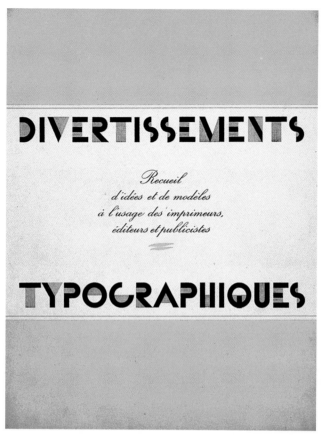

244

245

246

247

248

244-245. DIVERTISSEMENTS TYPOGRAPHIQUES, *periodical covers, c. 1933. Designer: Maximillien Vox.*

246-248. VARIOUS SAMPLES, *printing specimens, c. 1933. Designers unknown.*

249

250

FRANCE

Freedom in French typography was found in advertising layouts and modern posters, in which A. M. Cassandre said the letter was "the leading actor." In the Modern French poster, every visual element revolved around the word, and often the word revolved around the poster as a frame. The result was integrated compositions where type served as a surrogate illustration. The letters were bold, geometric, and stylishly unique to the age. Cassandre wrote that he was inclined "not toward a parody of inscription but toward a pure product of the T-square and compass, toward the primitive letter." Since its inception in the days of Fournier and Didot, French typography has been known for its elegance, and this continued through the Modern era. French alphabets of the 1930s had grace and style, or, as the typographer Samuel Welo wrote, "the 'chic' so typical of the French people." Fonderies Deberny & Peignot went to great lengths to promote the functionality of its chic specimens through its periodical *Divertissements Typographiques,* edited by Maximillien Vox. The publication gave designers at the art studios of *les grands magasins* and printers a generous sampling of the latest releases. It was actually a portfolio of loose examples of commercial job printing using the foundry's most popular faces. Typographers were also invited to sample faces as a loss leader against the larger sale of complete fonts of hot metal.

249. PARIS LIEGE, *travel poster, 1930. Designer: J. P. Junot.*

250. AVROGÈNE, *hand-lettered logo, c. 1933. Designer unknown.*

251-256. DEBERNY & PEIGNOT, *type catalog, 1926. Designer unknown.*

FRANCE

Through beautiful specimen books, innovative booklets, and startling posters, Fonderies Deberny & Peignot induced printers, typographers, and designers to sample its unequalled bounty of metal types. The quality of the inventory matched the quantity. For example, Cochin, designed in the late nineteenth century by Nicolas Cochin and redrawn and cut in the early twentieth, was one of the company's most popular French faces for many decades. It was marketed through a lavish multipage booklet replete with many tip-ins of actual applications. But these small typographic displays were mere supplements to the annually published, two-volume type catalog featuring both traditional and contemporary typefaces, including Bifur, Peignot, Photo, Film, Europe, and Éclair. These smartly designed books featured a tabular indexing system (common for industrial catalogues but unique in the type trade) and were the perfect printer's companion. The books set a standard that other foundries attempted to match. It becomes very apparent from the printed ephemera of this period that the French had a passion for letter forms—the good, the bad, and the outlandish. During the period between the two world wars, France was perhaps only second to the United States in the amount of commercial printed material released to the public.

257

258

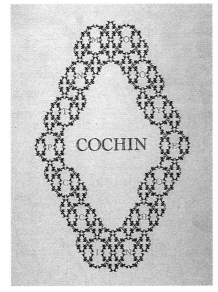

259

260

257. AUX GALERIES LAFAYETTE, *billhead, 1923. Designer unknown.*

258. DELEPOULLE, *billhead, 1929. Designer unknown.*

259-260. COCHIN, *type specimens, 1912. Type designer: Charles Nicolas Cochin.*

UNITED STATES

"If we don't watch out we will spend half of our time arguing about what 'modern' means," wrote Edmund G. Gress, editor of *The American Printer*, in 1930. In an article titled "Typographic Styles Change Every Generation," he referred to his specific era as the "Modern Phase," yet asked the rhetorical question: "What is present-day typography?" At the time, the modern idea was tied to dynamic asymmetry, flow lines, and abstraction. Gress suggested that "the reader might get the impression that a word or ornament is glued on each buckshot and then fired from a gun onto the surface of the paper." So-called modernism was looked upon with great suspicion as well as a lack of understanding, so Gress spoke up for the European Moderns: "modernists talk of disregarding all tradition and laws of design and typography, and doing things in a free and original manner, with the result that some take their words literally, and there are typographic chaos and anarchy." He reassured traditional printers that Modern typography is rooted in "the thou-shalts and thou-shalt-nots, and the really good piece of modern typography is fairly simple and sane." The New Typography was dedicated to order. Commercial modernism was dedicated to show.

261-262. RALEIGH INITIALS, *type specimen, 1930. Type designer: Willard T. Sniffin.*

263. VULCAN, *type specimen (Linotype), 1929. Type designer: K. Sommer.*

264. 9TH ANNUAL OF ADVERTISING ART, *book jacket, 1930. Designer: A. Welp.*

265. LOESER'S, *catalog cover, 1928. Designer unknown.*

266. THE GREENWICH VILLAGE QUILL, *periodical cover, 1929. Designer: H. Fowtz.*

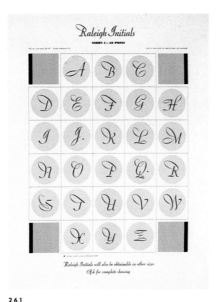

261

262

263

264

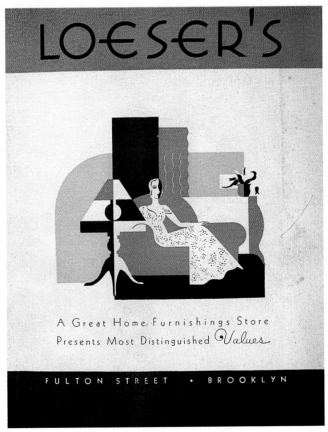

265

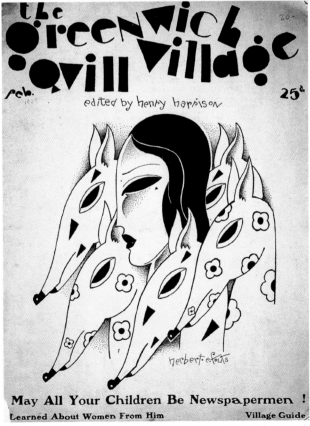

266

A B C D E
G H K M
L N O R
S T V W

268

"Modern typography owes much to its charm, subtlety, and expressiveness . . . " wrote Frederic Dannay in "How to Use Modern Display Types" in 1931. "The practicability of a type selection is as vital to typographic correctness as distinctive 'atmosphere.' An inharmonious color tone, a misfit size, an illegibility in mass, will transform the most appropriate 'feeling' into the most incongruous effect." Many admonishments were published in the trade press to prevent printers from raucousness. With the unprecedented number of new typefaces issued by American producers such as the American Type Founders (ATF), Continental Type Founders, Bauer Type Founders (USA), Linotype, Ludlow, and Intertype, the tendency was to design "modern" layouts with undisciplined abandon. Dannay listed rules that he believed would eliminate the threat of type pollution: "don't use a typeface merely because it is the later importation from Europe; don't use a hand-lettered headline if there is a typeface that suits your purpose *just as well*; typography, like style, works in cycles; don't use unnecessary rules, borders or decorations." He concluded, "Only the expert layout man can take advantage of a practice which offers so many pitfalls."

269

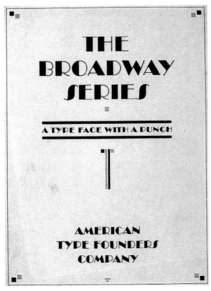

270

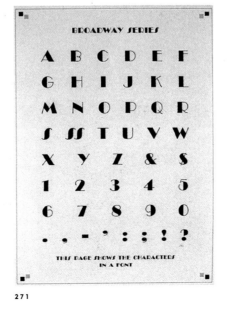

271

267. MODERNISTIC, *type specimen, c. 1932. Type designer: Samuel Welo.*

268. BERNHARD TANGO AND SWASH CAPITALS, *specimen sheet, 1934. Type designer: Lucian Bernhard.*

269. GALLIA SERIES, *type specimen, 1927. Type designer: Wadsworth A. Parker.*

270–271. THE BROADWAY SERIES, *type specimen, 1929. Type designer: Morris Fuller Benton.*

UNITED STATES

Despite continued use of European imports, type was nationalistic in the United States. The reasons vary: The expense of physically importing heavy metal fonts across the ocean was high; American commercial needs differed from those in Europe; and the applied-art traditions were very different. Although the New Typography was achieving more widespread acceptance by the early 1930s, the original European ideal was not the American way. Edmund Gress wrote, "I am keen for Americanizing this modern movement, and one way to help is to base what we do on American motives." But what Gress determined was required to bring Modernism into the fold had more to do with decoration than philosophy. "Use metallic bronze ink in silver and gold and copper on printed work where tint blocks or heavy-printing type faces are used," he suggested. "Metallic surfaced paper and cardboard also fit in as a background for modern typography." The standard bearers of deco were acutely aware that too many faces were on the market, so trade journals suggested relying on a few current ones. The *American Printer* advised, "Seriless types that are the vogue . . . are examples of attempts to eliminate non-essentials, and these attempts are successful when the letters have historic proportions or have grace of design," and urged that new sans serifs replace old Gothics in "printer's permanent equipment."

272-273. THE NUBIAN SERIES, *type specimen, 1928. Type designer: Willard T. Sniffin.*

274-275. UNTITLED ALPHABETS, *type specimens, c. 1928. Designer: Samuel Welo.*

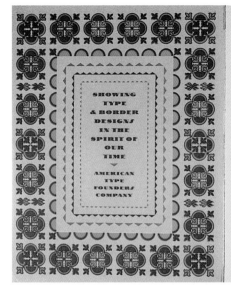

272

273

274   275

276

277

278

279

276. NOVEL GOTHIC, *type specimen,*
1929. Type designers: Charles Herman
Becker / Morris Fuller Benton.

277. BETON, *type specimen (originally*
a German typeface), 1934. Type designer:
Heinrich Yost.

278. SPHINX, *type specimen (originally*
French), 1928. Designer unknown.

279. ULTRA-MODERN, *type specimen, 1928.*
Type designers: Douglas C. McMurtrie,
Aaron Borad, Leslie Sprunger.

280

281

ABCDEF,GHIJKJ
LMNOPQRSTUV

282

ABCDEFGHIJKL
MNOPQRSTUV

283

ABCDEFGHI JKLMNOPQR STUVWXYZ

284

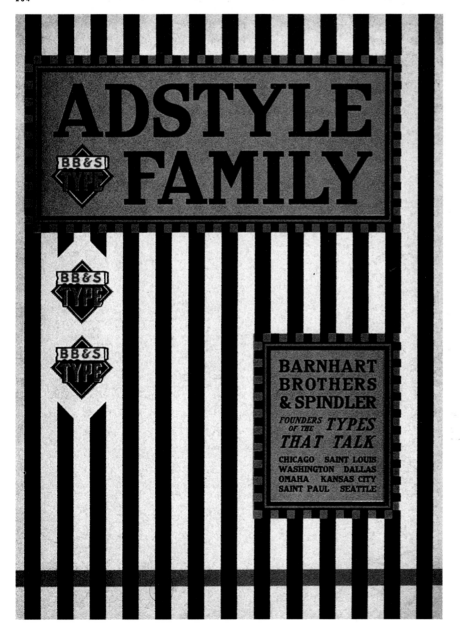

285

"The word 'modern' has worried us not a little," wrote Alice Beeson Ecke, a production specialist at *Harper's Bazaar* in a 1930 issue of *The American Printer*, "for it seems to have been such an excellent excuse for the pretender to call himself an artist. And, like the other applied arts, 'modern' typography, with but few exceptions, has been in the hands of the pretenders and for a time fell into a sorry state. It expressed nothing but a blur of type and rules, an ugly mixture of Roman and Gothic types—all labeled, in large letters 'MODERN.'" This was the common complaint in the 1930s because not all type designers and typographers remained true to the highest standards. Grace and elegance were not always the concern of commercial artists who created signs and "shocards," the goal of which was to grab the attention of passersby quickly and without artifice. The majority of the ephemeral typefaces that bore the stigma of "fake modernism" were designed by decidedly competent professionals whose job was to create novelties in current styles for advertising and promotion. To call these types Modern is stretching the term. The types used for mass-market display had roots in the modernistic, streamline style.

280. SIGNS, *title page for sign book, 1936.*

281. CAROL'S, *sample from sign book, 1936.*

282. INLINE OUTLINE, *alphabet (variation on Zepplin by Rudolf Koch), c. 1930.*

283. EXPRESSIONIST, *alphabet (variation on Neuland by Rudolf Koch), c. 1930.*

284. CHOP SUEY, *alphabet, c. 1935. Type Designer: Ross F. George.*

285. ADSTYLE FAMILY, *type specimen, 1906 & 1920. Type designer: Sydney Gaunt.*

GERMANY

German type design was even more fervently nationalistic than that of other nations. Blackletter already set the Germans apart from countries using Roman type; yet as universal as promoters professed the New Typography rebellion to be, the Modern style was still Germanic in the strictures that governed its application. The German approach could be rigid, but the leading German type foundries, among them Stempel, Flinsch, Berthold, Klingspor, and Bauer, were in the business of producing and selling commercially popular typefaces, and thus willing to diverge from nationalist traditions. In addition to Blackletter, two forces influenced German type design of the early twentieth century: The first was *Sachplakat*, which inspired the reevaluation of antique letterforms as well as introduced *Plakatstil* (poster style) typefaces. Second, German Modernism had a major impact on typography by the mid-1920s, as seen by the shift in preference among printers from antique to sans serif type designs. Paul Renner's Futura was the paradigm, but other, more quirky, sans serifs were introduced for novelty sake. Trade magazines that reluctantly supported New Typography promoted less austere variations.

286

287

286. NEISCH PLAKAT FARBEN, *advertisement, c. 1925. Designer unknown.*

287. UNTITLED, *alphabet, 1930. Type designer: Paul Klein.*

288-291. VARIOUS LETTERHEADS, *c. 1925. Designer unknown.*

292. AN ALLE, *advertisement, c. 1928. Designer unknown.*

293. IM KAMPF, *advertisement, c. 1928. Designer unknown.*

288

289

290

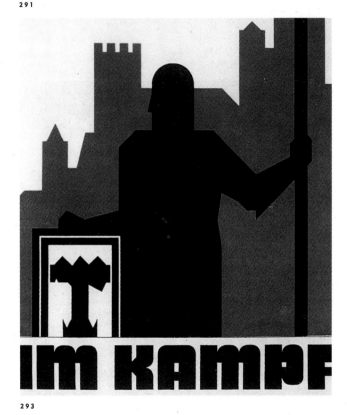

291

292

293

294

295

296

297

298

299

GERMANY

Deco type design was a marriage of old and new. The major demand of the average German printer and sign painter was for alphabets that would set often similar messages off from one another. Blackletter, even the decorated variety, was not the most eye-catching style for use on the street, where most people were exposed to commercial pitches at a fast rate and in quick succession. Literally taking a page out of common sign-painters manuals, type designers developed entire new alphabets from letters used on window and wooden commercial signs. The examples reproduced here were, in fact, redrawn from these sources and collected in a copyright-free portfolio available to journeyman *Gebrausgrafikers* (commercial artists) who wanted to add a bit of color and verve to their otherwise mundane messages. For these display letters, color was further added to give the illusion of depth and dimension. One of the appeals was that these letters virtually jump off the printed page. The faces ran the stylistic gamut from faux scripts with inlines and outlines to altered Gothics with shadows and highlights. Some of the alphabets conform to the prevailing international styles, while others have a decidedly antique German sensibility with references to Blackletter. Some were given distinctive names, but most were simply generic contemporary forms. Nor were they proprietary; *Gebrausgrafikers* were encouraged to redraw directly from these specimen sheets.

294-300. FARBIGE ALPHABETS, *type specimens, c. 1932. Type designer: Otto Heim.*

GERMANY

During October 1925, when members of the German Printers' Association opened their monthly issues of the printing and type industry journal *Typographische Mitteilungen*, they were unprepared for a shock. The conventional layout of small margins and tightly packed Fraktur body type was replaced by avant-garde composition with sans serif type and bold red and black rules. Overnight the comfortable style that dominated commercial printing had been replaced by anarchy. In fact, Jan Tschichold had been invited to edit an issue, and he introduced German printers and typographers to avant-garde typography as practiced in Russia, Holland, East Europe, and Germany. The cover of the issue was empty of all but the most essential ornament; the interior layout was a little crude, with a lot of white space and replete with sans serifs. This issue was only a blip, however, a short detour from the norm. The following month *TM* returned to its usual format. Although *TM* was the first official journal to introduce the New Typography, it did not follow or further support its orthodoxy. It did, however, become force of moderation, balancing the avant-garde and the status quo by promoting deco type and lettering as a viable compromise. The majority of German designers represented by this and other official trade organizations may have been truly inspired by the exemplars of Modernism, but they did not play an active role in its continued development. Regardless, Tschichold's issue of *TM* is today a cherished artifact, while the other issues are forgotten.

301

302

303

301. RICH & RUHNAY, *letterhead, 1925. Designer unknown.*

302. REKLAME PLAKATE, *advertisement, 1924. Designer unknown.*

303. TITLE, *alphabet, 1930. Type designer: School of Decorative Art, Stuttgart.*

304. TYPOGRAPHISCHE MITTEILUNGEN, *periodical cover, 1925. Designer unknown.*

TYPO GRAPHISCHE MITTEILUNGEN

ZEITSCHRIFT DES
BILDUNGSVERBANDES
DER DEUTSCHEN
BUCHDRUCKER
HEFT

4

APRIL 1925 × XXII. JAHRGANG

SPAIN

In the Spanish Republic during the late 1920s, Deco became the unofficial national graphic style that linked Spain to the rest of industrialized world. Such graphics were used inside Spain to promote many of the same products and services that signaled progress elsewhere, and on Spanish products outside the country to project a comparable standing with other leading nations. Originally, printers took responsibility for the production of advertisements and posters, but eventually designers became creators of visual form while printing concerns were transformed into advertising agencies. In Barcelona, advertising became a commercial necessity, and what began as a craft-oriented, anonymous profession adhering to mundane typographic convention became a wellspring of unprecedented design experimentation. The introduction of modernistic mannerisms to typography in the early 1920s was a means of grabbing the consumer's attention. Although comparatively few original typefaces emanated from Spain, designers customized many contemporary foreign alphabets. For the most part, Spanish type foundries imported faces from France, Germany, and England. French decorative tendencies and German rationalist ideas were wed to Spanish type. Yet this was also a period when many of the most emblematic letter forms on posters and brochures were drawn by hand.

305. NOVADAM, *advertisement, 1931. Designers: Estaban Trouchut Bachmann and Juan Blanchard.*

306. PUBLICIDAD, *type specimen, 1930. Designer: F. T. José Iranzo.*

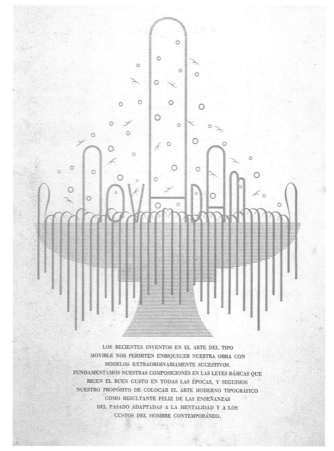

LOS RECIENTES INVENTOS EN EL ARTE DEL TIPO
MOVIBLE NOS PERMITEN ENRIQUECER NUESTRA OBRA CON
MODELOS EXTRAORDINARIAMENTE SUGESTIVOS.
FUNDAMENTAMOS NUESTRAS COMPOSICIONES EN LAS LEYES BÁSICAS QUE
RIGEN EL BUEN GUSTO EN TODAS LAS ÉPOCAS, Y SEGUIMOS
NUESTRO PROPÓSITO DE COLOCAR EL ARTE MODERNO TIPOGRÁFICO
COMO RESULTANTE FELIZ DE LAS ENSEÑANZAS
DEL PASADO ADAPTADAS A LA MENTALIDAD Y A LOS
GUSTOS DEL HOMBRE CONTEMPORÁNEO.

305

306

307

SALA DE FIESTAS
Plaza Tirso de Molina, 1
TELÉFONO 70600
MADRID

308

309

RELOJERÍA ESPAÑOLA, S.A.

ADUANA, 26-28   TELÉFONO 10131

SAN SEBASTIÁN

310

311

307-310. VARIOUS LETTERHEADS, *specimens, c. 1934. Designers: Estaban Trouchut Bachmann and Juan Blanchard.*

311. PERFUMES Y ESENCIAS, *certificate, 1930. Designer unknown.*

ITALY

Rejecting any semblance of symmetry, the Futurist's *parole in libertà* (words in freedom) simulated on paper the sounds of excited speech and the noise of whirring machines. In the early 1920s, Futurists created their own forms of avant-garde advertising "events," and these new approaches moved quickly off their manifestoes and into mass commercial art. Fortunato Depero introduced an array of dynamic hand-drawn letters that symbolized speed and motion. Saw-edged and rectilinear, stair-step gothic types begun as improvisations soon developed into fully realized and commercially available alphabets. From posters for automobiles, cigarettes, and liquor to Fascist party documents and propaganda, Italian graphic designers used contemporary typefaces to appeal to youthful consumers. Despite the growth of a totalitarian government that dressed itself in the trappings of ancient Rome, the rise of moderne design as public communication took the edge off the dictatorial strictures of the regime. Typographic standards were routinely challenged, yet in Italy, the birthplace of humanist type, ancient type tradition was taken very seriously. Futurism's rejection of the past had great influence on many designers, but modernism was not monolithic. Some designers also preferred venerable scripts, and Romans in the spirit of *Italianismo* were also fairly common.

312

313

---

312. V FIERA, *advertisement, 1937. Designer: R. Antore.*

313. III MOSTRA MARINARA D' ARTE, *postcard, 1929. Designer: Latini.*

314. TALCO BORICO FLORENTIA, *bookmark, c. 1925. Designer unknown.*

314

315

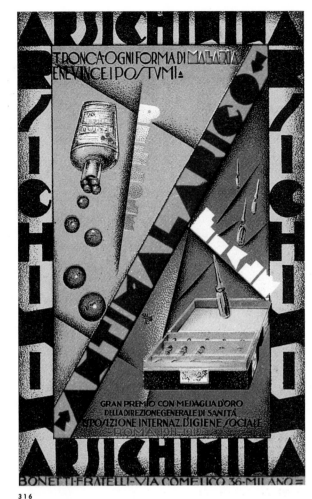

316

317

318

319

315. BOLOGNA-FIRENZE, *booklet, 1934.*
Designer unknown.

316. ANTIMALARICO, *postcard, c. 1925.*
Designer unknown.

317. FA LA CORTESIA, *sheet music, 1926.*
Designer: Onorato.

318. LE GRANDI FIRME, *periodical*
cover, 1928. Designer unknown.

319. COMOEDIA, *periodical cover, 1921.*
Designer: Santi.

320

321

322

323

324

THE NETHERLANDS

Dutch Deco was exuberant and colorful. Commercial Modern type design there was a combination of various *au courant* influences. First was the proto-avant-garde *Wendingen* style, an eccentric decorative typography used in the arts and architecture magazine of the same name that was developed as the signature of designer H. Th. Wijdeveld. Essentially rectilinear, this type was designed as if on a grid, but with quirky angles and indentations like the contours on a map. A second influence was de Stijl and the box-like type originally designed by Theo van Doesburg, built entirely on the foundation of a square. Some of these letters were rigid and entirely void of any ornamentation. The modern typefaces imported from France and Germany, both the austere and the ornamented, were a final influence. The combined use of all these styles ultimately defined this phase of Dutch commercial design. The use of all large and small capitals, however, underscored the Dutch contribution to the overall pan-European style. The most renowned artifacts of Dutch graphic design today are examples of the New Typography by Piet Zwart and Paul Schuitema, but the overwhelming majority of print design for commercial purposes in the Netherlands between the wars was modernistic. Type foundries in Holland, like in the rest of Europe, produced decorative inline and outline typefaces in large quantities because they were most in demand, and commercial job printers conformed to the standard usage of these faces as found in trade magazines devoted to contemporary advertising.

320. KUNST, *periodical cover, 1932. Designer unknown.*

321. RADIO EXPRES, *periodical cover, 1938. Designer unknown.*

322. WENDINGEN, *periodical cover, 1930. A. P. Smits.*

323. STALEN THONET MEUBELEN, *advertisement, 1932. Designer unknown.*

324. FLORA BISCUITS, *advertisement, 1930. Designer unknown.*

EASTERN EUROPE

Many of the most common East European Deco typefaces originated in Germany and were distributed through satellite outlets in the East. Futura was probably more widespread in Czechoslovakia, for example, than in Germany at the time because Czech printers were encouraged by their professional organizations to emulate *au courant* approaches. Advertisements in trade journals celebrated Futura as the symbol of modernity. Other European typefaces—serif and sans serif alike—were often customized with the appropriate accent marks, yet few other modifications separated the types from one nationality to the other. This does not mean that these East European countries shared exactly the same methods. The Modern design movements in East Europe all had distinctive points of view. In addition, each nation had traditions of printing and design with long bloodlines. Some members of the printing dynasties retained the classical methods, while others both adjusted to the changing styles and maintained their links to craft and artistry. Commercial modernism developed out of a need for mass communication, but in Czechoslovakia, Hungary, and Poland the standards of printing and typography were not sacrificed because of the increase in ephemeral printing.

325

325. PATRONA GROTESK, *type specimen, 1928 (Czechoslovakia). Designer unknown.*

326. KÁLDOR, *advertisement, 1932 (Hungary). Designer unknown.*

327-330. VARIOUS TYPOGRAPHERS, *advertisements, 1932 (Hungary). Designers unknown.*

326

Szállít: Teljes nyomdaberendezéseket, tömöntödei berendezéseket és dobozgyártási berendezéseket

SCHELTER & GIESECKE A/G

LEIPZIG C1

111 évóta gyártja: a világhírű Phönix tégelysajtót, 2 turás Windsbraut gyorssajtót, 1 turás Wetlläufer gyorssajtót, lehúzóprést, nyomóautomatákat, számozógépet kézi és lábhajtásra, önműködő számozószekrényt bármily géphez, számozóművek teljesítmény ellenőrzéséhez minden géphez. Elsőrendű betűket a világ minden nyelvéhez, fabetűket, trolitbetűket, körzeteket, hangjegyeket, értékpapir nyomáshoz teljes berendezést, minden nagyságban klisékét 2, 3, 4 szin nyomáshoz a legjobb kivitelben, mindennemű klisék raktáron, galvánok rotációsgéphez, regálisok, szekrények, teljes faberendezések, könyvkötő betük aranyozópréshez is, domborító anyagok és vésetek.

Rézléniák, rézkörzetek, sorzók (winkelek), szedőhajók.

MAGYARORSZÁGI KÉPVISELŐ: FISCHER IGNÁCZ BUDAPEST, VI., PRÓFÉTA-U. 9 TELEFON: AUTOMATA 199—07

Záróstégek, forma- és fazettastégek, sarokvágógépek, reglettavágók, zsebméterőszalag cicerós és centiméter beosztással, korrektúralehúzógépeket, stb

327

linotype

a legmodernebb a legrégibb és a legeredményesebb **szedőgép**

LUDLOW betűsoröntőgép

ELROD lénia- és reglettaöntőgép

GUTENBERG-HÁZ GEEL TESTVÉREK

Képviseli: Molkenthin Gusztáv Budapest VII, Rombach-utca 8 Telefonszám : Automata 42-9-09

328

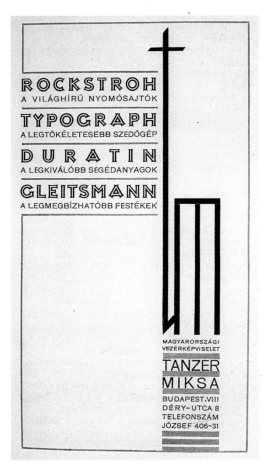

ROCKSTROH
A VILÁGHÍRŰ NYOMÓSAJTÓK

TYPOGRAPH
A LEGTÖKÉLETESEBB SZEDŐGÉP

DURATIN
A LEGKIVÁLÓBB SEGÉDANYAGOK

GLEITSMANN
A LEGMEGBÍZHATÓBB FESTÉKEK

MAGYARORSZÁGI VEZÉRKÉPVISELET

TANZER MIKSA

BUDAPEST, VIII DÉRY-UTCA 8 TELEFONSZÁM JÓZSEF 406-31

329

KÖNYVKÖTÉSZETI MUNKÁK: Diszkötések, brosurák, üzleti és szállítókönyvek • Présaranyozás és minden e szakmába vágó munkák a legtökéletesebb kivitelben, a legjutányosabb áron NYOMDAI BÉRMUNKÁK: Lapoknak és nyomtatványoknak kikészítése • • Litográfiai munkák szakszerű vágása • Lyukasztás, öznirzés, bigelés, sarokvágás különböző nagyságban

KERTÉSZ KÖNYVKÖTÉSZET
BUDAPEST V, VISEGRÁDI-UTCA 23 TELEFONSZÁM: AUTOMATA 911-98

330

EASTERN EUROPE

The Czechs nurtured many original designers, like Anton Jero, who softened Modernism through the addition of witty graphic images. The Hungarians had Alexander Bortnyik, a follower of the Bauhaus, and A. Berény who wed Modern type and moderne illustration into functional yet decorative art. The Poles spawned many modernistic designers at the Szkole Prezemyslu Graficznego in Warsaw. Typography was practiced throughout these countries with great attention to tradition and with an eye to the current market. This growing market ensured that constant type replenishment was an important aspect of the printing industries. The French exported full fonts, but the Germans made the largest contribution to the typecases. When West Europe foundries opened branches in these countries, type was manufactured there as well. The trade journals admonished their readers not to misuse the styles, which was indeed common wherever type was used. One journal developed a guide to the most popular dos and don'ts. It suggested, for instance, that Rudolf Koch's Neuland, which gives the charm of a woodcut, should be used only in association with "airplanes, automobiles, books, coffee, and steamship lines and cruises." As for Renner's Futura, only the inappropriate uses were listed: "'heavy' products, like tractors, and old fashion products."

331. THALWIESER, *advertisements, 1932 (Hungary). Designer unknown.*

332. VILIMOVSKY, *poster, c. 1935 (Czechoslovakia). Designer: Bratrí Vilimovsky.*

333. POLSKI, *advertisement, 1932 (Poland). Designer: Z. Kmiecik.*

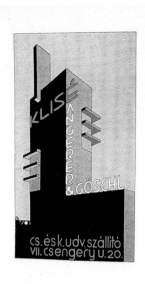

331

332

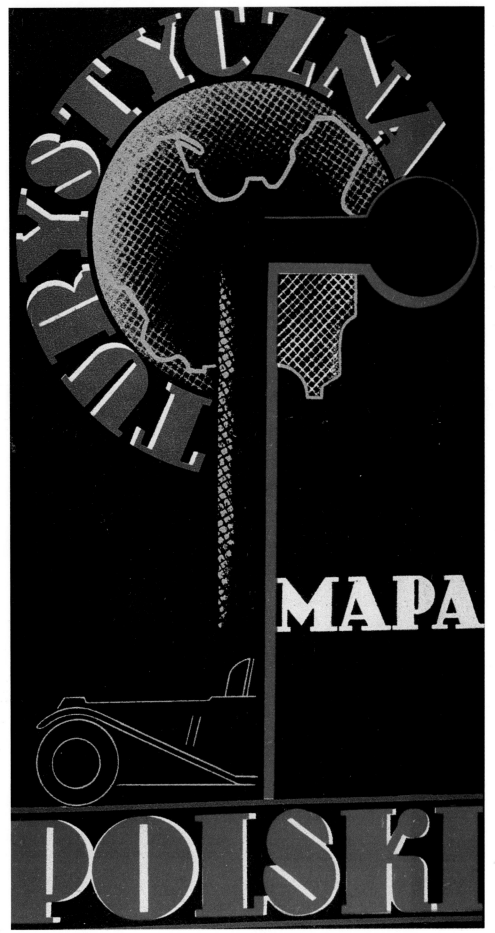

internationale
bürofachausstellung
basel
29. sept.–15. okt. 1928
mustermessgebäude

büro

L A T E M O D E R N

The beginning of the end of the rebellious laboratory phase of avant-garde Modernism in Europe began in 1928, when Stalin imposed Socialist Realism and outlawed Constructivism in the USSR. Then, in 1933, Hitler closed the Bauhaus; the Nazis also rejected sans serif type as *Judenlettern* and temporarily replaced it with Fraktur, the "German type." Although the leading Bauhaus type masters, Laszlo Moholy-Nagy and Herbert Bayer, brought the Bauhaus spirit to the United States, the transplanted New Typography merged with more eclectic and less rigid American sensibilities into Late Modernism. By 1940 Jan Tschichold entirely renounced the dogma of the New Typography and returned to classical design models. With the outbreak of World War II, there was little time for new type design; and, dependent on scarce resources, manufacture itself was limited. During the 1940s, sophisticated American typography—the work of Paul Rand, Alvin Lustig, Lester Beall, and Bradbury Thompson—was influenced by the "old" New Typography with a native twist. Sans serifs were popular and Futura prevailed, but these were often complemented by Bodoni, Garamond, and Caslon romans

and italics; Modernism's hard edges had been removed. Type was also designed to speak or illustrate the messages it was conveying. Conversely, in postwar Switzerland, the other terminus of the Modernist diaspora, the New Typography evolved into a more reductive, purely functional form exemplified by *Neue Grafik* (new graphic design) typefaces like Akzidenz Grotesk, Bücher-Grotesk, and Gill. These were used in asymmetrical layouts for both legibility and dynamic impact, or what Josef Müller-Brockmann referred to as reflecting "the tensions of modern times." With the introduction of Univers (1954) and Helvetica (1956) in Switzerland and its subsequent worldwide distribution, Late Modern was characterized by economy—white space dramatically contrasted with the printed surface. During the postwar decades, this evolutionary phase of Modernism, also known as the International Style, was known for its ubiquity in corporate communications and advertising.

OPPOSITE: BÜRO, *poster, 1928. Designer: Theo Ballmer.*
ABOVE: KNOLL + DRAKE FURNITURE, *advertisement, 1954. Designer: Ladislav Sutnar.*

SWITZERLAND

The proponents and exponents of Modernism took safe haven Switzerland. The Swiss School, or International Typographic Style, of the early 1950s directly descended from the avant-garde, specifically de Stijl, the Bauhaus, and the New Typography. The progenitors, Theo Ballmer and Max Bill, had studied typography at the Bauhaus, and they retained the philosophical aim to achieve objective clarity, rather than individualistic style, in printed communications. Their work of the late 1930s and early 1940s prefigured the reductive functionality that characterized the movement. The basic principles that both Ballmer and Bill espoused were that layouts be constructed of geometric elements and organized mathematically. In the late 1920s, Theo van Doesburg issued a manifesto calling for a universal art of absolute clarity based on arithmetical standards. Accordingly, geometric spatial divisions—the grid—and Akzidenz Grotesque type, a well proportioned variant of a turn of the century sans serif, were key components in early Swiss design. The grid method introduced strict hierarchies of typographic import that revolved around a concept of using only one type style (in one or two weights) in the same layout. Importance was addressed not only in terms of the relative point size or weight of the type, but by its position on the grid. Although ad hoc grids are invisibly present in most classical design, the overt application of modular grids, geometric progressions, and sequences were codified and sanctified through the International Style.

334

335

336

334. INTERNATIONAL ZEITUNG, *poster, 1960. Designers: Gerstner & Kutter.*

335. HELVETICA, *type specimen, 1956–57. Type designers: Edouard Hoffman and Max Miedinger.*

336. NEUE GRAFIK, *periodical cover, 1960. Designer: Carl Vivarelli.*

337. UNIVERS, *type specimen, 1954. Adrian Frutiger.*

338. INCABLOC, *advertisement, c. 1953. Designer: Gottfried Honegger.*

339. WILHELM TELL, *poster, 1963. Designer: Armin Hofmann.*

340. DIE ZEITUNG, *poster, 1958. Designer: Emil Ruder.*

univers   *univers*

univers   *univers*

univers   *univers*

337

338

Basler Freilichtspiele
beim Letziturm im St. Albantal
15.-31. VIII 1963   Wilhelm Tell

339

Gewerbemuseum Basel
Ausstellung «die Zeitung»
9. April bis 18. Mai 1958
Geöffnet
werktags 10-12 und 14-18
sonntags 10-12 und 14-17
Eintritt frei

die
Zeitung

340

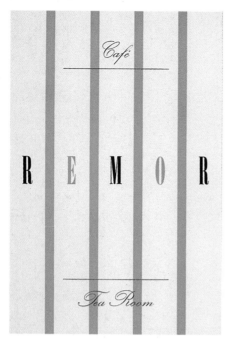

Café

REMOR

Tea Room

341

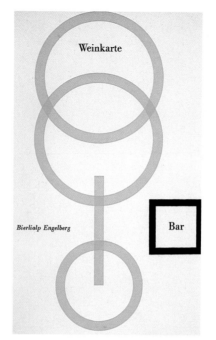

Weinkarte

Bierlialp Engelberg

Bar

342

Dancing

Huguenin

bar

Restaurant

343

Eisen
Meyer+Co
bau

Luzern   Gibraltarstr. 24   Telefon 26202

344

HOTEL   GOTTHARD   WEGGIS

wein

karte

345

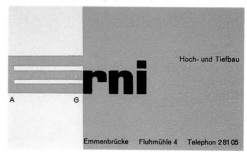

Hoch- und Tiefbau

rni

A   G

Emmenbrücke   Fluhmühle 4   Telephon 2 81 05

346

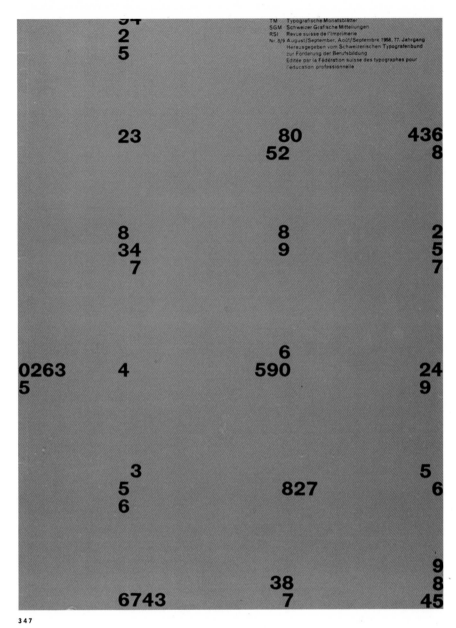

347

ALBERT BRUN   HERGISWIL AM SEE   TELEPHON (041) 2 04 76   POSTCHECK VII 2538

MÖBEL-SCHREINEREI

brun

348

341-346. VARIOUS BUSINESS CARDS, *c. 1948. Designers: Walter Bangerter & Walter Marti.*

347. TYPOGRAFISCHE MONATSBLÄTTER, *periodical cover, 1958. Designer unknown.*

348. BRUN, *letterhead, c. 1953. Designers: Walter Bangerter & Walter Marti.*

SWITZERLAND

The Swiss style was not monolithic. Differences in approach were apparent in Basel and Zurich, and in their two design schools, where the International Typographic Style flourished. At the Gewerbeschule in Basel, Emil Ruder taught a typography class that experimented with the contrasts, textures, and scale offered through Univers. He wrote a 1967 book, *Typography: A Manual of Design*, which explored how to achieve a wide range of texture variations while limited to this single font. Armin Hofmann, another Basel school faculty member, evolved a philosophy based on the elemental language of point, line, and plane, and replaced the designer's pictorial reliance with dynamic harmony of typographic elements. He also wrote a book in 1965, *Graphic Design Manual*, that was a manifesto of elementary principles. In Zurich, teachers at the Kunstgewerbeschule, including Josef Müller-Brockmann and Carlo Vivarelli, used photographic imagery, but continued to proffer type structures rooted in objectivity—"universal graphic expression." Zurich was also the base for the magazine *Neue Grafik* (New Graphic Design), founded in 1959, which showcased the movement's accomplishments in interior, industrial, and graphic design. Its format was based on a mathematical grid, and the size, weight, and positioning of the type indicated its hierarchy. The magazine expressed the essence of Swiss typography. From the 1950s to the 1970s, multinational corporations agreed that the dynamic neutrality of the Swiss style was effective graphic communications.

GERMANY

The postwar repository for the Bauhaus spirit was located in the city of Ulm, at the Hochschule für Gestaltung (Institute of Design). This complex of buildings and dormitories was established to experiment with and produce new forms of industrial and graphic design; it also attracted students from all the industrial countries. Max Bill contributed to the curriculum; other formulators were type designers Otl Aicher and Anthony Froshaug, each of whom brought a rationalist sensibility to typography. While the Swiss method was built upon mathematical principles, the Ulm school went a step further into the scientific realm by introducing semiotics—the theory of how signs and symbols operate in the communications environment—into the curriculum. The school also required that students explain their respective rationales. The result was type devoid of individualism, but dynamic in a universal sense. The Germans were not, however, oblivious to the humanistic aspect of typography in everyday life. "Typography. . . reflects our linguistic culture, warts and all," wrote Aicher, who continued to distinguish the differences between objective and subjective typographies: "Writing has rhetorical forms, modes of expression, just like speech. We must differentiate, however, between writing that seeks to convey meaning and writing that strives to produce diverse forms of articulation." The Ulm typographic program allowed for variation within the parameters of objectivism. Helvetica was the type of choice, for it was meant to be universal, clean, and rational.

349

349. GEBRAUCHSGRAPHIK, *periodical cover, 1954. Designer unknown.*

350. GEBRAUCHSGRAPHIK, *periodical cover, 1952. Designer: Herbert Bayer.*

351. GRAPHIK, *periodical cover, 1950. Designer unknown.*

350

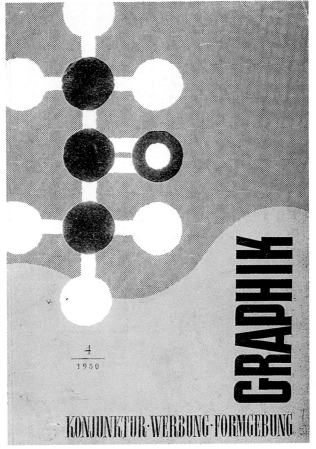

351

352

353

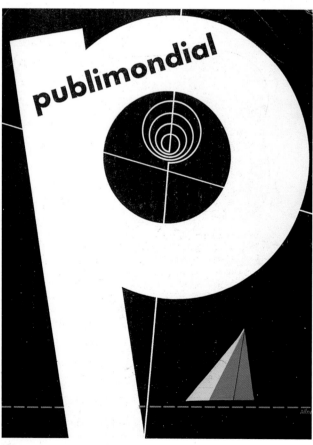

354

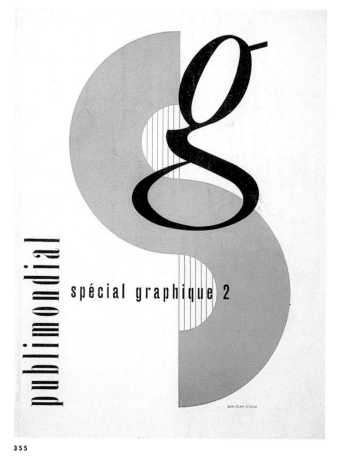

355

356

352-355. PUBLIMONDIAL, *periodical covers, 1948–52. Designers: Eveleigh-Dair, P. Fix-Masseau, Walter Allner, Jean Picart LeDoux.*

356. BIFUR, JACNO, LE FILM, BANCO, ETOILE, *type specimens from the type foundry Deberny & Peignot, c. 1954.*

FRANCE

Charles Peignot, proprietor of Fonderies Deberny & Peignot, was so deeply committed to producing contemporary typefaces that he financed the research of both the earliest attempts at phototypesetting technology and the development of Adrian Frutiger's Univers. He also advocated international standards of typographic manufacture and quality. For the better part of the early postwar years, however, France did not contribute further to the International Style; it was a follower not a leader. This is not to say that novel type design was entirely forsaken, nor that remarkable graphic design was totally absent. The poster was still alive and well. French Late Modernism was not influenced by the objective or scientific methods found in Switzerland or Germany, but instead evolved a pictorial approach based on a marriage of illustration and text, just as it had in the 1920s and 1930s, when A. M. Cassandre, Paul Colin, and Jean Carlu, among other *affichistes*, produced innovative poster designs and alphabets to go with them. This was in large part because quotidian advertising, rather than corporate identity systems, was the leading graphic design genre in France. Advertising required more distinctive type and typography than the universal styles. To make the advertising genre contemporary, some aspects of Swiss and German Modernism were applied, but France, being France, did not profess fealty to the grid in the same way. Contemporary French type design was at once based on prewar designs and interested in making them functional in new communications contexts.

THE NETHERLANDS

In 1933, the Bauhaus was established anew in Chicago as the New Bauhaus. Likewise in Amsterdam, the New Art School carried on Bauhaus traditions. Until the Nazi occupation, Holland was very hospitable to avant-garde design. After the war, Holland was primed for revitalized design. Amsterdam and The Hague were where type experimentation was put into practice, its leading pre-war designers—Zwart, Schuitema, and others—had introduced avant-garde notions to major Dutch businesses and corporations, which continued to be receptive after the war. The Dutch government, especially the PTT (postal, telephone, and telegraph) was an enthusiastic patron of graphic design that transcended the commonplace, and designers took responsible license to fulfill the communications requirements set forth. During the postwar period, the PTT was (and is to the current day) the wellspring of progressive ideas. Another was the Stedelijk Museum, whose design director, Willem Sandburg, continuously experimented with type, printing techniques, and paper stocks, the combination of which he saw as important for the overall communication. His typography for *Experimenta Typografica* was inspired by the formal teachings of the New Art School and the less formal machinations of "underground" printer/designers who had produced ad hoc messages in opposition to the Nazi occupation. He created striking contemporary posters. At the same time, for his experimental work, he used type as abstract form, denoting a dichotomy between formal and intuitive Modernists.

357

357-363. EXPERIMENTA TYPOGRAFICA, *booklet, 1956. Designer: Willem Sandburg.*

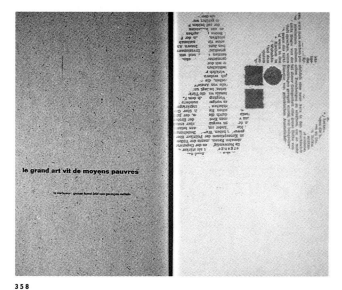

le grand art vit de moyens pauvres

le corbusier   grosse kunst lebt von geringen mitteln

358

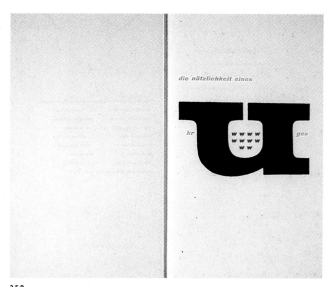

die nützlichkeit eines

kr ü ges

359

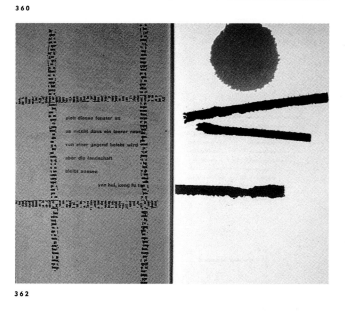

lao tse behauptet

dass einzig + allein im vakuum das wahrhaft bedeutungsvolle ruhe

die realität eines zimmers   ruhe z.b. im leeren raum

der vom dach + wänden   umschlossen sei nicht in

dach + wänden selbst   die nützlichkeit

eines wasserkruges   wohne in seiner leere

in die das wasser   hinein gegossen werden

könne – nicht in der   form des kruges

oder im material aus   dem er hergestellt sei

im leeren raum allein wird die bewegung möglich

kakuzo okakura   das buch vom tee

360

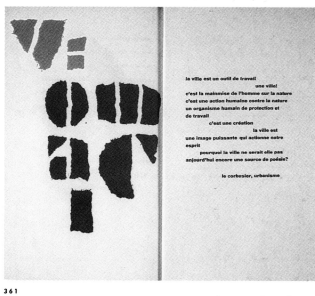

la ville est un outil de travail
                             une ville!
c'est la mainmise de l'homme sur la nature
c'est une action humaine contre la nature
un organisme humain de protection et
de travail
              c'est une création
                        la ville est
une image puissante qui actionne notre
esprit
       pourquoi la ville ne serait elle pas
aujourd'hui encore une source de poésie?

                le corbusier, urbanisme

361

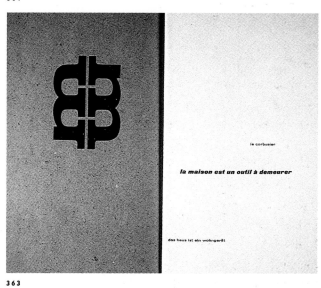

sieh dieses fenster an

es macht dass ein leerer raum

von einer gegend belebt wird

aber die landschaft

bleibt aussen

yen hui, kong fu tse

362

le corbusier

la maison est un outil à demeurer

das haus ist ein wohngerät

363

139

skill

Half a loaf may be better than no bread, but that's all that can be said for it. We of Davis, Delaney take a similar view of half-skill and half-quality. We can also provide all of those services prelusive to printing: design, typography, engraving. This mailing piece, executed to order, is a modest illustration.

lived, so the story goes, and not so long ago, an old man who made wondrously precise ship models. He was a master craftsman, an artist of the first order, a genius of infinite patience. For example, no model bearing his name ever had a solid, carved hull. His ships were built as ships properly should be built: the keel laid down, the planks steamed on. When he turned out a frigate, the inch-long guns could be fired, there was shot in the lockers, powder in the magazines, and the compass showed true north. Collectors, of course, fought for his work. One millionaire devotee travelled from San Francisco to Nantucket to offer the old man a four-figure bonus for the privilege of being allowed to buy one year's output. The old man looked at him and spat reflectively on a pile of wood shavings. "Mister," he said, "I don't work for money alone. I work for liking what I'm doing, and liking doing it well." War or no war, manpower shortage or not, true skill is always available.

364

365

366

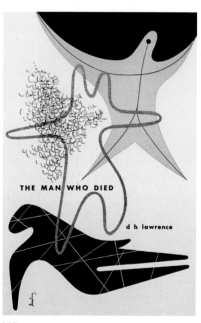

THE MAN WHO DIED

d h lawrence

367

364. SKILL, *brochure, 1948. Designer: Alexander Ross.*

365. PM, *periodical cover, 1937. Designer: Lester Beall.*

366. AD, *periodical cover, 1941. Designer: Paul Rand.*

367. THE MAN WHO DIED, *book jacket, 1949. Designer: Alvin Lustig.*

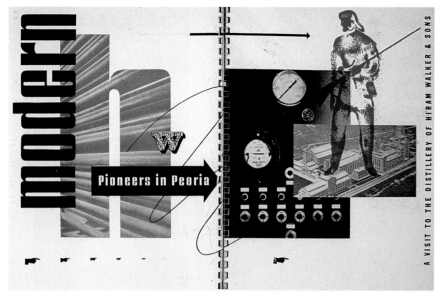

368

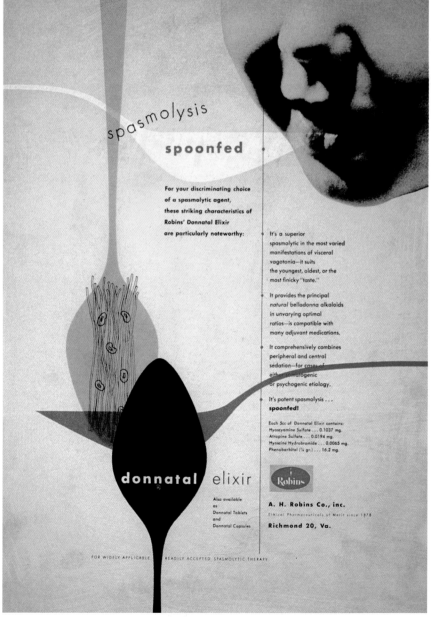

369

UNITED STATES 1940s

Modernism arrived in the United States via Europe, first through foreign trade publications and later with immigrant designers fleeing war and oppression. Paul Rand, America's leading Modernist graphic designer, discovered avant-garde Modernism in the early 1930s, when he saw Bauhaus graphics in a British trade journal; from that moment on, he accepted it as his typographic language. Rand admired the direct force of unsentimentalized expression, yet he was frustrated by the fact that these methods were not being taught at his or any other art school at the time. Instead, if it were taught at all, "Modernism" in American commercial art was reduced to a few conceits lifted from the pages of *The New Typography*, including asymmetrical layout and sans serif type. But the style was practiced without the moral underpinning of the Europeans, reducing Modernism to little more than a style of the moment. Perhaps given the American penchant for frequent changes of product veneers, this faux Modernism was little more than a fleeting fashion. For Rand, Lester Beall, Alexey Brodovitch, and others, however, Modernism was bolstered by a belief in the rightness of form and underscored by the idea that good design—fine typography and rational layout—would have a positive impact not only on the quality of printed matter, but on the quality of life.

368. MODERN PIONEERS IN PEORIA, *advertisement, 1935. Designer: Lester Beall.*

369. DONNATAL, *advertisement, 1948. Designer: Alexander Ross.*

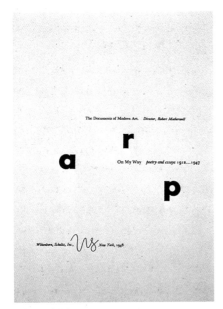

370

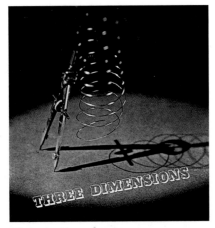

371

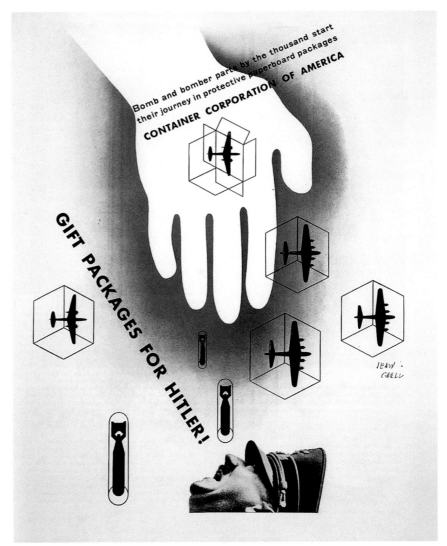

372

370. A R P, *title page, 1946. Designer:
Paul Rand.*

371. T H R E E D I M E N S I O N S, *brochure
cover, 1946. Designer: Dave Chapman.*

372. G I F T P A C K A G E S F O R H I T L E R,
*advertisement, 1943. Designer:
Jean Carlu.*

373. A G U I D E T O L E S T E R B E A L L,
*brochure cover, 1951. Designer:
Lester Beall.*

373

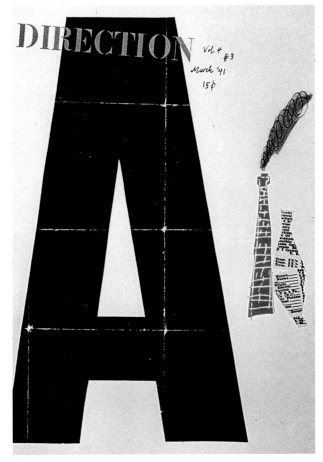

374

375

UNITED STATES
1940s

The key designers who worked at this time brought different influences to bear: Lester Beall was inspired by Dada, his work a mixture of abstract and antique elements. Will Burtin was interested in the layering of picture and text to communicate multiple messages. Bradbury Thompson found that classical type could be a viable component of the modern layout. Paul Rand was influenced by modern art as the basis for modern design. Each contributed to six principles of American modern typography that Eugene M. Ettenberg listed in his 1947 handbook, *Type for Books and Advertising:* 1. *Texture:* Use of enlarge, hard or soft, rough or smooth, surfaces . . . effecting our tactile senses via the eye . . . 2. *Juxtaposition:* Contrasts in subject or design. Combining unrelated illustration techniques and odd combinations of historical subjects with commonplace objects. 3. *Color:* Flat areas of sophisticated colors . . . 4. *Graphic effects:* Visual tricks, such as optical illusions, plays of light and shade, new angles, patterns of light. X-rays and photograms. 5. *Montages:* Creating illusions of proximity or distance, using reversed perspective. Cutting out subjects and pasting them into entirely new surroundings to give natural or supernatural impressions. 6. *Directional Movement:* Used to create action, tension or repose; balance or a disturbed equilibrium. Asymmetric layouts giving motion, throwing you forward, sensation of movement.

374-375. DIRECTION, *periodical covers, 1941, 1942. Designer: Paul Rand.*

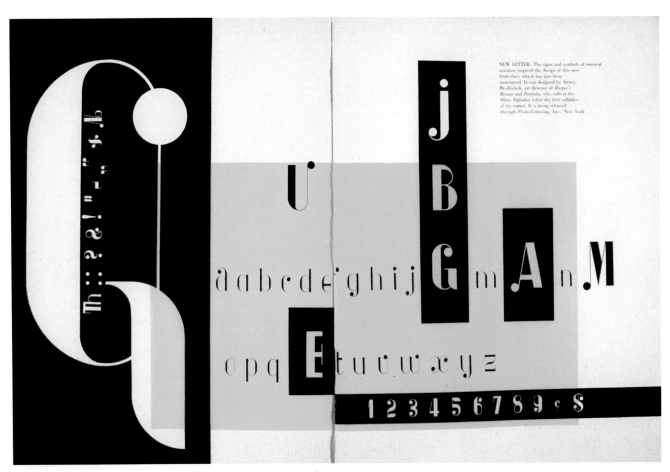

376

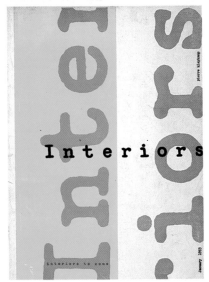

377

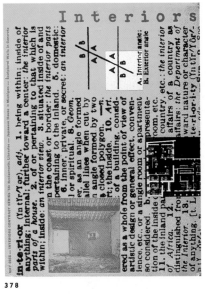

378

379

---

376. NEW LETTER, *experimental alphabet, 1950. Designer: Alexey Brodovitch.*

377-378. INTERIORS, *periodical covers, 1953, 1956. Designer: Pierre Kleykamp.*

379. DESIGN QUARTERLY (WALKER ART CENTER), *periodical cover, 1966–67. Designer: Peter Seitz.*

UNITED STATES
1950s/1960s

Individual designers maintained distinct type preferences—some were loyal to Futura, News Gothic, or Akzidenz Grotesque; others used Beton, Girder, and Stymie. A few mixed scripts, Baskerville, or Garamond with gothics. Foundries issued various sans serifs, including Bernhard Gothic (Lucian Bernhard) and Metro Black (W. A. Dwiggins), to offer variations in color and weight. The early Modern period was noted for being typographically dark in tone, but by the early 1950s, one type critic wrote, "Today the better designers who employ the principles of modern typography in advertising have made it shed its teutonic heavy-handedness." Although the progressivism of European avant-garde Modernism was respected by young American designers, by the postwar years it was received as a foreign culture with distinctly different commercial requisites. For Modernism to work in the American marketplace, it had to shed the dogma yet retain the progressive spirit. Reversing his own ideological claims, even Jan Tschichold renounced the dogmatic rules of the New Typography. Nevertheless, the ideals that were fronted by such typography were still valid. American designers maintained that they had a mission to make the print environment more beautiful and to convey information in a clear and accessible manner. Type design and typography were components of the larger mission.

380-383. WATCHING WORDS MOVE, *booklet, 1954, Designer: Robert Brownjohn.*

384. A, *Westinghouse font, 1962. Designer: Paul Rand.*

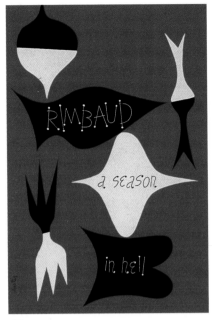

385

386

EVERYDAY ART

published by the american crayon company

387

ARE APPLES PECULIARLY, ESPECIALLY, EXCLUSIVELY OR EVEN CHARACTERISTICALLY AMERICAN?

388

NORTHERN SPY
JONATHAN
GRIMES GOLDEN
WINESAP
BEN DAVIS
RED ASTRACHAN
WEALTHY
HUBBARDSTON
LADY
EARLY JOE
GOLDEN PIPPIN
HOWARD BEST
CRANBERRY PIPPIN
MAIDEN BLUSH
PRIDE OF GENESEE
GLADSTONE (HAPPY ROCK)
PHILADELPHIA SWEET
CHENANGO

389

385. A SEASON IN HELL, *book jacket, 1948. Designer: Alvin Lustig.*

386. CATALOG DESIGN, *catalog cover, 1955. Designer: Ladislav Sutnar.*

387. EVERYDAY ART, *periodical cover, 1953. Designer unknown.*

388-389. THE LOVE OF APPLES, *brochure for the Composing Room, 1959. Designer: Gene Federico.*

390-391. THAT NEW YORK, *brochure for the Composing Room, 1959. Designers: Brownjohn, Chermayeff & Geismar.*

392. ADDO-X, *hang tag, 1954. Designer: Ladislav Sutnar.*

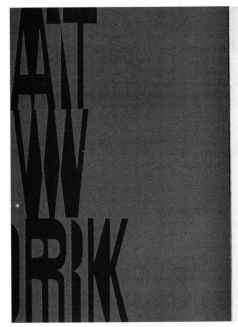

390

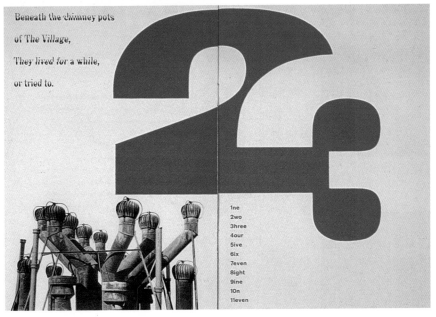

391

the "addo-x" model 2341E | an automatic multiplier at conventional adding machine cost

392

UNITED STATES
1950s/1960s

Modern American graphic design had utopian undertones, although in practice most designers were concerned with making design more accessible to the audience or receiver. Typographers sought to remove ambiguity from layouts to effect a clear, clean, and objective message. "Type should be read," wrote designer Erik Nitsche. "Too often . . . type is referred to as color. This is not wrong in itself, but leads to the next step which is to regard it as some grey matter which in turn can be cut up with scissors." While new ways of making typographic layouts often relied on artistic methods of composition, such as cut-and-paste collage of textures and blocks of color, during this time typography was finding new rationalist equilibrium. Indeed, the word became more prominent than before, especially in advertising, and typography became the instrument for communicating the clever (and memorable) headlines and slogans written for the so-called "Big Idea" advertisements that typified the 1950s creative revolution. During the early days of American advertising, slogans also triumphed over picture, but this contemporary emphasis on the word was not the same. Words conveyed ideas, but a new typography was essential. "The attempt to integrate pictorial and typographical elements is paramount," wrote Paul Rand. "By contrasting type and pictorial matter the design is able to create new relationships and new meanings." And Nitsche added that "Too often . . . titles are set for pictorial satisfaction only." Which is not the function of type.

UNITED STATES
1950s/1960s

The Creative Revolution in advertising, which began in the early 1950s, was a new phase of Modernism and a new era of type. The Composing Room, a New York type shop, fostered experimental type in the Modern tradition. What today can be called Late Modern typography, distinguished by the clean and simple compositions of both classical and modern typefaces, was changing the look of advertising from chaotic to eloquent; at the same time, it was more expressive. Bradbury Thompson promoted the concept of talking type: by tweaking traditional letter forms into visual puns, typeset words became both verbal and visual. This idea was pursued further by Robert Brownjohn, who imbued letters with sound and motion, making them into visual components of a word or phrase. Ivan Chermayeff went a step further in layouts where otherwise static type was made to appear kinetic in print. The letter form as pun was tested in advertising by Gene Federico, Lou Dorfsman, and Herb Lubalin. With precisionist care, Federico made type and image into a total composition. Dorfsman used type not only to state a message, but to perform it: Typeset words were totally integrated components of rebus-like compositions. Lubalin also exploited the type-as-sound idea and further proffered the sculptural eccentricities and pictorial potential of letter forms to their utmost communicative advantage.

393. 26 GOOD REASONS, *brochure, 1969. Designer: Herb Lubalin.*

394. THE MEDIUM IS THE MASSAGE, *book jacket, 1967. Designer: Quentin Fiore.*

26
GOOD
REASONS
TO USE
LBC

393

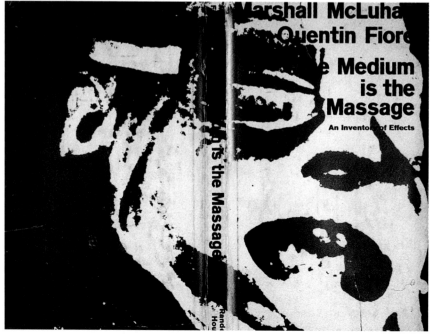

394

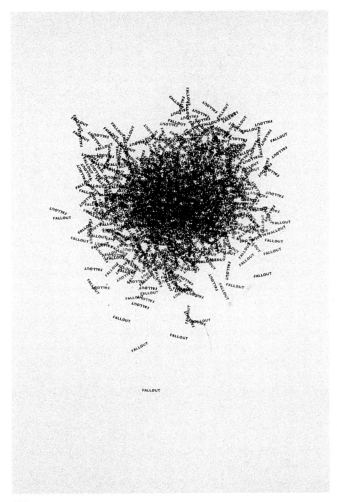

395

396

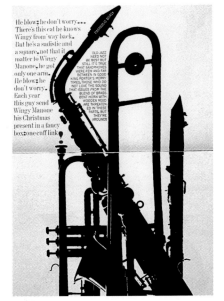

397

398

399

---

395. FALLOUT, *type experiment, 1957. Designer: Aaron Burns.*

396. GOMILLION VERSUS LIGHTFOOT, *book cover, 1962. Designer: Rudolph de Harak.*

397-399. JAZZ, *brochure for the Composing Room, 1959. Designer: Herb Lubalin.*

400

401

402

403

404

---

400. A I G A, *periodical cover, 1965.*
Designer: Thomas Geismar.

401. COMMERCIAL ART (CA), *periodical cover, 1960. Designer: Ivan Chermayeff.*

402. C R A W MODERN, *type specimen, 1958–64. Type designer: Freeman Craw.*

403. F O L I O, *type specimen, 1957–62. Designer: Walter Baum.*

404. V E N U S, *type specimen (Wagner & Schmidt Foundry, 1931). Revived by Bauer Type Founders, 1972.*

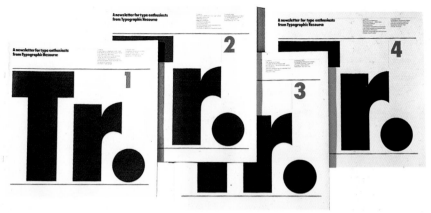

405

news gothic with | news gothic bold

THE COMPOSING ROOM, INC., 130 W. 46 ST., NEW YORK 36, N.Y. JUDSON 2-0100

406

UNITED STATES
1970s

Phototype altered the way designers, typographers, and type designers would forever practice. In the 1930s, phototype was occasionally used for headlines, but in the 1970s, as ad agency type directors turned more exclusively to phototype, its use became stylistically and compositionally more eclectic. The boundaries that separated orthodox Modernism from fervent eclecticism also began to blur. Two businesses, Photo-Lettering Inc. and International Typeface Corporation (ITC), encouraged pushing the boundaries of design and expanding the definitions of type play. The former was a repository for thousands of film faces (many new and novel, some classic and common) used primarily as headlines for advertisements and in periodicals. The Photo-Lettering specimen book was a typographic bible. The latter company marked a shift from foundry to independent distributor. ITC fonts were licensed to a growing number of companies, such as Visual Graphics Corporation, which introduced the Phototypositor. Aaron Burns was a leader of this transitory period. At the Composing Room, he bent the rules of hot metal, then as cofounder of ITC, he introduced the emblematic faces of the era, including Lubalin's Avant-Garde. Faces designed for Phototype proved that type was not locked into strict Modernism.

405. TYPOGRAPHIC RESOURCE, *catalog covers, 1978. Booklet designer: Bart Crosby.*

406. NEWS GOTHIC, *type specimen (originally designed in 1908 by Morris F. Benton), 1971. Booklet designer: Aaron Burns.*

UNITED STATES
1970s

By the mid-1970s, most corporate, institutional, and civic clients maintained some semblance of the International Typographic Style because it was neutral yet symbolized the zeitgeist. Advertising and editorial users, however, were beginning to expand into more eclectic typographic territory; but rather than relying on nostalgic revivals of once passé forms of type design, the new diversity was characterized by an adaptation of typographic history, finding little-known passé faces and making them thoroughly contemporary. Type design was a fairly specialized activity; its practitioners had to be skilled not only at conceptualizing but also at drawing the face to accommodate all conceivable permutations. Among the leading designers were Freeman Craw (Craw Clarenden, Craw Modern), Ed Benguiat (Benguiat, Benguiat Gothic), and Tom Carnase (Carnase). Each affixed their name to faces that were emblematic of the times. In addition, this was a period when customized hand lettering—featuring scripts, swashes, and ligatures—was very popular among art directors. Herb Lubalin designed headlines and body text as pictures of the words communicated. The 1970s had a distinct but variegated look; clean yet expressive, the word and image combined as one. Considering the long span between moveable type and phototype, this era lasted a mere nano second in the continuum. By the time phototype was accepted and hot metal was extinct, the next big sea change since Gutenberg's invention of moveable type had come.

407

408

---

407. AVANT GARDE LIGATURES, *type specimen, 1970. Type designers: Herb Lubalin and Tom Carnase.*

408. TYPEFACES DESIGNED BY BENGUIAT, *type specimens, 1978, 1975, 1970, 1974. Type designer: Edward Benguiat.*

409. BELL CENTENNIAL, *telephone directory page, 1978. Type designer: Matthew Carter.*

Vandiver Jerry D teleph 400 Office Park Dr --- 877-5538
　Res 5029 Kerry Downs Rd --- 967-8955
Vandiver John Henry 2712 Fairfax Av Besmr --- 425-8805
Vandiver K D 1610 12th S --- 328-7604
Vandiver P A Jr 364 Midwood Av Midfld --- 923-9106
Vandiver Post Office Vandvr --- 672-9302
Vandiver Richard W 1506 Warrior Rd --- 788-0677
Vandiver Ronald 126 2nd Av S --- 324-5735
Vandiver W P LtCol 1548 Bessmer Rd --- 923-1283
Vandiver William 1610 12th S --- 328-7604
Vandiver Willie Rev 5418 11th Av Wylam --- 780-8599
Vandiver Willie J 524 54th Fairfld --- 780-0243
Vandrell Richard L 1420 66th W --- 923-5922
Van Drimmelen Cays 223 Green Park South --- 979-2260
Van Dusen & Atkinson Inc
　1800 Ave K Lipscomb --- 428-2621
Van Dusen M K Route 3 Warrior --- 647-7033
Van Dusen Paul L 3617 Haven Hill Dr --- 956-0177
Van Dyke E W 1324 Oak Terr --- 854-3491
Vann Hoyt 1232 Frisco Wylam --- 786-2571
Vann J Mason 118 Vann Hueytown --- 491-2644
Vann J Thompson 1882 Montclair Ln --- 823-0590
Vann J W Riverlawn Resort --- 674-5270
Vann Jackie 1309 21st N --- 251-3098
Vann James A Jr 3201 Sterling Rd --- 879-4245
Vann James E Castle Heights --- 681-2523
Vann James J Jr 8303 5th Av N --- 833-3933
Vann James R 2204 Little Valley Rd --- 979-0984
Vann Jerry 1025 Rutledge Way --- 788-5058
Vann Jimmy C Morris --- 681-8134
Vann Joe K Mrs 1915 7th NE --- 854-4729
Vann John David 1853—C Arboretum Cir --- 823-0785
Vann John Thomas 1333 Orlando Cir --- 854-4729
Vann Johnnie 7748 4th Av S --- 838-1735
Vann K G Castle Heights --- 681-9857
Vann L K 1300 Warrior Rd --- 788-0284
Vann Larry A 716 Park Ln Fultndle --- 849-4206
Vann Lee 1904 May Cir Fultndle --- 849-7567
Teenager's Telephone
　1904 May Cir Fultndle --- 849-5159
Vann Leona 609 Forest Rd Hueytown --- 744-7512
Vann Lowell Dr 3472 Birchtree Dr --- 822-5442
Vann M L 913 13th Midfld --- 744-0773
Vann Mary E 221 13th Ter N --- 252-1735
Vardaman Earl 1216 58th S --- 595-2909
Vardaman G 3550 Altamont Rd --- 251-1516
Vardaman J I Wilsnvle --- 669-7312
Vardaman J J Jr 1529 Valley View Cir --- 879-7497
Vardaman James T
　905 Independence Dr Alabstr --- 663-7888
Vardaman Joyce
　1529 Valley View Cir Homwd --- 879-3106
Vardaman Kathi
　1529 Valley View Cir Homwd --- 879-3106
Vardaman Lela Mae 2021 Warrior Rd --- 787-1345
Vardaman M T 953 Beech Ln --- 879-5316
Vardaman Tom Frank 2831 Highland Av S --- 322-6491
Vardaman W K 8917 Roebuck Blvd --- 833-7112
Vardaman W W Camp Branch --- 663-9043
Vardaman William P Jr 836 Fancher Dr --- 979-6995
Varden Aubrey E
　2156 Pratt Hwy Crumley's Chapel --- 798-2829
Varden C L 909 Valley Ridge Dr --- 870-3443
Varden Colan J
　1916 Emerald Av Crumley's Chapel --- 798-0237
Varden Connie 4320 5th Av S --- 595-1094
Varden David D 709 Robin Av --- 798-8727
Varden Earl O Scenic Dr Gardndle --- 631-3271
Vasquez Jacquely 143 Cambrian Way --- 967-7774
Vasquez Richard P 143 Camrian Way --- 967-8561
Vassar Amos Rev 2422 Dartmouth Av Besmr --- 428-3693
Vassar E E Rev Almont --- 552-3357
Vassar Annie Pearl 112 40th Av N --- 665-1572
Vassar Kenneth Wayne
　4627 Huntsville Av Brighton --- 425-2809
Vassar Nellie Montevallo --- 665-5344
Vassar Pauline Miss 8609 Division Av S --- 836-4194
Vassar R M 917 N 11th Besme --- 425-4243
Vassar Clifton 330 11th S Basmr --- 424-0654
Vassar David 224 2nd Av S --- 251-3549
Vassar Fred 943 5th Pl W --- 251-5907
Vassar Jim 943 5th Pl W --- 322-3072
Vassar Virginia 609 5th Way Pratt City --- 798-6373
Vassiliou Constantine P Dr
　1303 Woodland Village --- 879-5678
Vassiliou John 136—D 25th Av NW --- 854-4325
Vassiliou William G 2717 Highland Av S --- 252-2477
Vatalaro M R 1917—L Treetop Ln --- 822-5251
Vath Joseph Most Rev 8131 4th Av S --- 833-0171
　Res 200 Tuscaloosa Av SW --- 328-0521

VAUGHAN---See Also Vaughn

Vaughan A B 2850 Fairway Dr E --- 871-2005
Valley Avenue Car Wash East 313 Valley Av --- 942-5376
Valley Avenue Plaza Coin Op Lndry
　416 Valley Av --- 942-9810
Valley Avenue Shell Self Service
　100 West Valley Av --- 942-7814
Valley Avenue Standard Service
　Station 101 Green Springs Hwy --- 942-8514
Valley Beauty Salon 1704 Oxmoor Rd --- 871-7622
VALLEY BOLT & SCREW CO
　Cahaba Valley Rd --- 967-2700
VALLEY BROOK APARTMENTS
　2912 Gallant Dr --- 854-0398
Valley Cabinets 3193 Cahaba Heights Rd --- 967-2410
VALLEY CHAPEL 1802 Oxmoor Rd --- 879-3401
Valley Chiropractic Center
　2031—A Canyon Rd --- 823-5931
Valley Christian Church 2600 Cherokee Pl --- 879-0419
Valley Cleaners 1911 Oxmoor Rd --- 879-1369
VALLEY DISTRIBUTORS 2067 Valleydale Terr --- 979-3363
Andrews Patricia 317 Exeter Av S --- 822-3660
Andrews Patricia 317 Exeter Av S --- 822-3660
Andrews Patricia 317 Exeter Av S --- 822-3660
Andrews Patricia 317 Exeter Av S --- 822-3660
Andrews Patricia 317 Exeter Av S --- 822-3660
Andrews Patricia 317 Exeter Av S --- 822-3660
Andrews Patricia 317 Exeter Av S --- 822-3660
Andrews Patricia 317 Exeter Av S --- 822-3660
Andrews Patricia 317 Exeter Av S --- 822-3660

VALLEY DRAPERY & RUG CO INC
　2200 2nd Av S --- 322-1684
Value Mart Dollar Store---
　5515 1st Av N --- 592-9220
Value Mini Mart 600 Forestdale Blvd --- 989-9069
Value Oil Company---
　Office 105 Vulcan Rd --- 942-4786
　Fultondale Station Highway 31 N --- 841-8819
　Pleasant Grove Station
　700 Pleasant Grove Rd --- 744-6021
Value Shoes 9430 Parkway East --- 833-0579
Value Super Mart 2800 Cherry Av Pratt City --- 674-7843

VAN---See Also Vann

VAM advo 586 Shades Crest Rd --- 823-0579
Van And Storage Co movers 5529 1st Av S --- 595-1108
Van Baalen Harold acct 1900 28th Av S --- 879-3521
Van Buren Isaac Zion Av Zion City --- 871-4119
Van A E 2909 Highland Av S --- 833-2468
Vance Albert L 4821 Powell Av S --- 252-8981
Vance Alice 332 Irving SHermn Hts --- 595-0286
Vance Alice M Pelhm --- 786-3654
Vanda Beauty Counselor --- 663-6740
　2008 Clb Dr NW Huntsville Ala --- 852-9616
　If No Answer Dial --- 595-0324
Vandagriff Nick 920 Colesbury Cir --- 663-4729
Vande Brake Robert 3500 Brookwood Rd S --- 967-7849
VanDeBurg Larry
　1416 King George Dr Alabstr --- 663-6331

VANDEFORD---See Also Vandeford

Vandeford J W Mrs 1412 55th Wylam --- 780-7095
Vandeford James 4400 Bessemer Super Hwy --- 428-6514
Vandeford Stella J Mrs 1728 34th Ensely --- 786-1298
Vandegriff Albert H 610 Av S --- 786-1298
Vandegriff D H 3808 10th Av S --- 592-4829
Vandegriff D H III 634 Camp Cir --- 836-0581

VANDEGRIFT---See Also Vandergrift

Vandegrift Ben Mrs 2500 Riverhaven Dr --- 822-2328
Vanderburg Ted
　Woodward Estates Mobile Home Park
　Lipscomb --- 428-5415

VANDERFORD---See Also Vandeford

Vanderford C B Mrs 1301 60th Central Park --- 923-0255
Vanderford Cecil L Flat Creek --- 674-9968
Vanderford Cleo 3144545 40th Pl N --- 841-0021
Vanderford John W 1324 11th Av S --- 324-2019
Vanderford Lillian K McCalla --- 477-6486
Vanderford O H 415 Shades Crest Rd --- 822-3230
Vanderford Rita 1010 Lorene Ct Bessmr --- 426-3327
Vanderford W E 2340 Chapl Rd Bluff Pk --- 822-3543
Vandergraff William H 1305 2nd Av --- 781-2855
Vandergriff B S 1519 29th Terr S --- 879-6369
Vandergriff Gary L 4700 74th Pl N --- 836-3594
Vandergriff I A teleph 600 19th St N --- 321-8222
　Res 637 Winwood Dr --- 622-6760

VANDERGRIFT---See Also Vandegrift

Vandergrift Charles A 956 Meg Dr --- 853-6097
Vaughan Tom B Jr Dr 3700 Dunbarton Dr --- 967-7482
Vaughan Uriah E Jr 3503 Clamont Dr Pinson --- 681-2622
Vaughan V H 1005 Herring Midfld --- 428-5194
Vaughan W B 840 Parkway Cir East Montvlo --- 665-1904
Vaughan W C 609 9th Av Midfld --- 785-3461
Vaughans Catherine L 205 West Brighton --- 428-2225

VAUGHN---See Also Vaughan

Vaughn A L 2216 2nd Av N Irondale --- 956-2964
Vaughn Allen C 2012—B Vestavia Park Ct --- 979-3982
Vaughn Arvel Coyce 334—A Vise Rd Pinson --- 681-6166
Vaughn B E 712 S 48th --- 592-3540
Vaughn H Melvin Dr ofc 2030 3rd Av N --- 254-3656
　Res 3808 Spring Valley Dr --- 967-5748
Vaughn Hamilton M Trafford Rd Trafrd --- 681-6755
Vaughn Harry C Jr ins 15 Office Park Cir --- 854-7986
　Res 2494 Dolly Ridge Trail --- 822-2171
Vaughn Harry Insurance Inc
　15 Office Park Cir --- 879-7920
Vaughn Henry F 4210 Parkway Fairfld --- 786-7090
Vaughn Homer 2616 Ridgebrook Rd --- 841-0525
Vaughn Howell L Montvlo --- 668-1419
Vaughn J W 603 Hillcrest Rd --- 681-3934
Vaughn Huey J County Line Rd --- 787-1648
Vaughn Hunter G 308 Church Forst Hls --- 780-2581
Vaughn Hunter G 35 Five Hundred Row --- 854-0188
Vaughn J A 120 Town And Country Cir --- 836-6191
Vaughn J C 619 Ridge Rd Roebuck Springs --- 251-1851
Vaughn Lamar 2302 10th Ct S --- 798-0297
Vaughn Jack B 2824 Thornhill Rd --- 871-4413
Vaughn Jake R phar 585 Shades Crest Rd --- 822-1210
　Res 2120 Vestavia Dr --- 823-1134
Vaughn James
　Sharon Heights Mobile Home Park --- 674-6230
Vaughn James C rl est 528 20th N --- 322-3325
Vaughn Willie Jr 511 Virginia Gardndle --- 631-8997
Vaughn Woodrow 6401 Court F Fairchld --- 787-4749
Vaughner Arma 1413 28th N --- 251-6065
Andrews Patricia 317 Exeter Av S --- 822-3660
Andrews Patricia 317 Exeter Av S --- 822-3660
Andrews Patricia 317 Exeter Av S --- 822-3660
Andrews Patricia 317 Exeter Av S --- 822-3660
Andrews Patricia 317 Exeter Av S --- 822-3660
Andrews Patricia 317 Exeter Av S --- 822-3660
Andrews Patricia 317 Exeter Av S --- 822-3660
Andrews Patricia 317 Exeter Av S --- 822-3660
Andrews Patricia 317 Exeter Av S --- 822-3660
Andrews Patricia 317 Exeter Av S --- 822-3660
Andrews Patricia 317 Exeter Av S --- 822-3660

Vaught Donald L 542 39th St Short Wylam --- 780-8608
Vaught Ernest 65 Merrimont Rd Hueytown --- 491-6244
Vaught J C 625 Barclay Ln --- 836-2436
Vaught Joe Jr Stertt --- 672-2919
Vaught Ralph L 700 77th Wy S --- 836-8452
Vaught Susan A 2109 46th Pl Central Pk --- 787-4227
Vaultz Eva 1543 Dennison Av SW --- 925-1752
Vause S F 603 Huckleberry Ln --- 979-5289
Vause Stephen F 445 Shades Crest Rd --- 823-2662
Vautier Harold G 204 Killough Sprngs Rd --- 853-5626
Vautrot Ruby L Mrs 2021 10th Av S --- 933-2265
Vazquez Norberto Old Jasper Hwy Adamsvle --- 674-3370
Veach J L 5725 Belmont Dr --- 956-3990
Veach Loren Aldrich --- 665-1831
Veal Ad 4520 21st Av S --- 251-9049
Veal Ad rl est 1711 Pinson --- 841-7380
Veal B Evan atty 1711 Pinson --- 841-2789
Veal Clarence E Garndle --- 631-3856
VEAL CONVENTION SERVICES---
　1711 Pinson --- 841-2789
　2109 10th Av N --- 322-6102
Veazey W B Vincent --- 672-9506
Veazey Wilbur E 1541 53rd St Ensley --- 923-1960
Veazey William A 287—A Chastaine Cir --- 942-4137
Veazey Willie J 3084 Whispering Pines Cir --- 823-5795
Vebber Mark H 5216 Goldmar Dr --- 956-1661
Vebco contr 1900 28th Av S Homewood --- 879-2259
Vedel Dental Technicians inc lab
　1116 5th Av N --- 322-5475
Vedel George C 3848 Cromwell Av --- 967-2832
Vedel George C Jr 744 Saulter Ln --- 871-8234
　Res 34744 Saulter Ln --- 870-9758
Vedel Murrey B 612 Oakmoor Dr --- 942-3619
Vedell Collen J Daisy City --- 674-7772
Vedell William L 8830 Valley Hill Dr --- 833-9915
Veenschoten & Co mfrs agts 2930 7th Av S --- 251-3567
Veenschoten L A 1919—D Tree Top Ln --- 822-7109
Vega Abraham 915 16th S --- 871-8883
Vega Delores C—B Watertown Cir --- 933-7619
Vega Edwin 2116 Rockland Dr Bluff Park --- 836-5980
Vegetable Patch Number 1 The
　Highway 31 S Alabstr --- 663-7618
Vegetable Patch Office Alabstr --- 663-7378
Vegetable Patch The Number 2 Dogwood --- 665-4179
Veigl Patrick B Pawnee --- 841-1238
Veitch Beulah 1172 Five Mile Rd --- 853-3361
Vest W L 4708 Lewisbrg Rd --- 841-7402
Vest W T 4737 N 68th --- 836-6371
Vesta Villa Exxon Self Serve 1500 Hwy 31 S --- 823-5008
VESTAVIA AMOCO SERVICE
　1456 Montgomery Hwy --- 823-1213
VESTAVIA BARBEQUE & LOUNGE
　610 Montgomery Hwy Vestavia --- 822-9984
Vestavia Barber Shop
　610—A Montgomery Hwy --- 823-1974
VESTAVIA BEAUTY SALON
　710 Montgomery Hwy --- 823-1893
Vestavia Beverage Co 623 Montgomery Hwy --- 822-9847
VESTAVIA BOWL
　Montgomery Hwy S Vestavia --- 979-4420
Vestavia Church Of Christ
　2325 Columbiana Rd --- 822-0018
VESTAVIA CHURCH OF GOD
　2575 Columbiana Rd --- 823-1895
Vestavia Church Of God Day Care day
　nursry 2575 Columbiana Rd --- 823-1895
VESTAVIA CITY OF---See Vestavia
Hills City Of
VESTAVIA COIFFEURS
　617 Montgomery Hwy Vestva --- 823-1104
Vestavia Country Club---
　Shades Mountain --- 823-2451
　Golf Shop Shades Mountain --- 822-8300
　On Mondays & Before 8:30 AM Dial
　As Follows---
　Stable Shades Mountain --- 823-2451
　Accounting Dept Shades Mountain --- 823-2979
　Golf Course Supt Shades Mountain --- 823-2019
　Tennis Shop Shades Mountain --- 823-2689
　General Manager's Ofc --- 823-2139
　Building Maintenance Shop
　Shades Mountain --- 823-2349
　Swimming Pool Shades Mountain --- 822-2559
Vestavia Country Club Employee's
　Lounge Shades Mountain --- 822-9840
Vestavia Hardware & Home Supply
　593 Shades Crest Rd --- 823-1953
VESTAVIA HILLS BAPTIST CHURCH
　2600 Vestavia Dr --- 871-4661
VESTAVIA HILLS CITY OF---
　513 Montgomery Hwy --- 823-1153
　Fire Dept Business 513 Montgomery Hwy --- 823-1153
　To Report A Fire --- 823-1296
　Training Bureau --- 823-1153
　Preventive Bureau --- 823-1190
　Administrative Offices
　513 Montgomery Hwy --- 979-6410
　Mayor's Office --- 979-6410
　Police Dept Business
　513 Montgomery Hwy --- 823-1153
　Detective Division --- 823-1442
　Police Chief --- 823-1153
　Recreational Center 1973 Merryvale Rd --- 823-0295
　Schools---
　Superintendent Of Schools
　1204 Montgomery Hwy --- 823-0295
　Pizitz Middle School---
　Office 2020 Pizitz Dr --- 823-0423
　Continued On Next Column

Andrews Patricia 317 Exeter Av S --- 822-3660
Andrews Patricia 317 Exeter Av S --- 822-3660
Andrews Patricia 317 Exeter Av S --- 822-3660

Continued From Last Column
　Lunchroom 2020 Pizitz Dr --- 823-0832
　Bandroom 2020 Pizitz Dr --- 823-0423
Vestavia Hills Elementary-East---
　2109 Parkview Pl --- 823-4900
Vestavia Hills Elementary-West---
　1965 Merryvale Rd --- 979-3030
Vestavia Hills Elementary---
　Lunchroom 2109 Parkview Pl --- 822-8632
Vestavia Hills High School---
　Principal's Office 2235 Lime Rock Rd --- 823-4044
　Assistant Principal's Office
　2235 Lime Rock Rd --- 823-4044
　Registrar's Ofc 2235 Lime Rock Rd --- 823-4044
　Physical Education Ofc
　2235 Lime Rock Rd --- 823-4130
　Bandroom 2235 Lime Rock Rd --- 823-2127
　Lunchroom 2235 Lime Rock Rd --- 823-4207
Street & Sanitation Dept
　2129 Montgomery Hwy --- 822-7289
　Garbage Pick-Up --- 822-7289
Vestavia Hills Cleaners
　1484 Montgomery Hwy --- 823-0874
Vestavia Hills Exxon
　732 Montgomery Hwy Vestavia Hls --- 979-3167
VESTAVIA HILLS PRIVATE SCHOOL
　1653 Shades Crest Rd --- 822-7289
Vestavia Hills United Methodist Church---
　2061 Kentucky Av Vestavia --- 822-9631
　Pastor's Study
　2061 Kentucky Av Shades Mountn --- 822-9021
Vestavia Homer E Memory Ln Hueytown --- 491-2180
Waldrop Ida B Mrs
　HolidayPark Trailer Court Besmr --- 426-5490
Waldrop Ida Oak Grove --- 491-2197
Waldrop J A 1975 East Bend Cir --- 853-8453
Waldrop J C 122 Houston Dr Brodmr --- 424-3190
Waldrop J D 3710—12 Bank St Brighton --- 424-4790
Waldrop J G 2536 6th Way NW --- 854-0340
Waldrop J W 3460 Manor Ln --- 871-0735
Waldrop Jack L 137 Forest Rd Hueytown --- 491-4676
Waldrop James 507 Sunrise Blvd Hueytown --- 491-1649
Waldrop James A New Bethel --- 647-9643
Waldrop James Caswell Sr Toadvine --- 436-3540
Waldrop James E 1617 Frontier Dr --- 822-3411
Waldrop James H
　3021 Allen Sheppard Dr Va Est --- 491-4172
Waldrop James O Harpersvile --- 672-7860
Waldrop James R 1129 Little John Ln --- 833-3091
Waldrop James R 3025 Teresa Dr Gardndle --- 631-7710
Waldrop James Robert 927 Valley Ridge Rd --- 871-0754
Waldrop James W Warrior Rd --- 436-3529
Waldrop James Woodrow
　157 Foust Av Hueytown --- 491-4787
Waldrop Janice rl est
　501 Riverchase Parkway East --- 979-1100
　Res 2300 Queensview Rd --- 822-4659
Waldrop Jerry W Howard Hill Dr Vincent --- 672-2536
Waldrop Jesse 5725 Ct M Central Park --- 923-9389
Waldrop Joe 6702 Forest Dr Fairfld --- 788-2115
Waldrop Joel H 1227 4th Av N Bessmr --- 428-8322
Waldrop John E 4123 40th Ct N --- 841-1541
Waldrop John R 133 Red Oak Cir --- 631-6535
Waldrop Johnnie Warrior River Rd Concord --- 491-9283
Waldrop Keith 314 Candy Mountain Rd --- 856-0984
Waldrop L R 107 Church Av Hueytown --- 491-2456
Waldrop L Ralph 3416 N 39th --- 841-3709
Waldrop Laddie S
　746 Goldenrod Dr Gardndle --- 631-5174
Waldrop Larry 2040 48th Pl Ensley --- 785-6079
Waldrop Lillian Mrs Wilsnvl --- 669-7367
Waldrop Luve 108 6th Robnwd --- 841-1796
Waldrop Lynne 1024 Basswood Cir Fultndle --- 631-6638
Waldrop M M 5612 12th Av S --- 592-9679
Waldrop Maggie L Dolmte --- 744-0727
Waldrop Maggie Lee Dolmte --- 744-8932
Waldrop Mendie Rockdale --- 424-0481
Waldrop Minnie
　312 Houston Saw Mill Rd Pinson --- 681-7506
Waldrop Myrtle B
　105 West Crest Rd Hueytown --- 491-6340
Waldrop Nora N
　Woodward Mobile Homes Est --- 426-2169
Waldrop Oscar N Dry Valley --- 665-4595
Waldrop P M 329 Roebuck Dr --- 836-2726
Waldrop Pamela 1444 Huffman Rd --- 853-8964
Waldrop Paul 245 Mabelon Ct Garywd --- 744-8282
Waldrop R G 4224 7th Av S --- 595-6771
Waldrop R Williams 116 Waverly Cir Lakwd --- 428-2965
Waldrop Ray 240 21st Av S --- 251-2699
Waldrop Richard D 724 Country Club Tr --- 631-9340
Waldrop Richard E Wilsnvle --- 669-6147
Waldrop Robert 132 8th Pleasant Grove --- 744-0222
Waldrop Robert C 75 Linden Cir Hueytown --- 491-1534
Waldrop Robert G ins 3055 Montgomery Hwy --- 879-8673
　Res 230 Lucerne Blvd --- 871-5313
Waldrop Robert M 120 Ski Lodge Dr --- 942-1157
Waldrop Robert R 1808 29th Av N Hueytown --- 491-7184
Waldrop Robert T 103 Midway Dr Hueytown --- 491-4533
Waldrop Ronald A 2047 White Post Rd Besmr --- 491-2055
Waldrop Ronnie
　115 Springdale Av Hueytown --- 491-7951
Waldrop Rosie 324 Houton Rd NW --- 681-8886
Waldrop Roy 3018 Warrior Rd Hueytown --- 744-0838
Waldrop Ruth 2816 29th Pl Ensley --- 788-8257
Waldrop S Ray 201 9th Av Besmr --- 425-6146
Waldrop Samuel G II 5000 Sunnydale Dr --- 491-4423
Andrews Patricia 317 Exeter Av S --- 822-3660
Andrews Patricia 317 Exeter Av S --- 822-3660
Andrews Patricia 317 Exeter Av S --- 822-3660
Andrews Patricia 317 Exeter Av S --- 822-3660
Andrews Patricia 317 Exeter Av S --- 822-3660
Andrews Patricia 317 Exeter Av S --- 822-3660

MAHALIA JACKSON

EASTER SUNDAY

PHILHARMONIC HALL

LINCOLN CENTER

Sunday, March 26, 1967 4:00 & 8:30 P.M.
TICKETS: 5.50, 5.00, 4.50, 4.00,
3.50, 2.95 Tickets Available at:
Lincoln Center Box Office &
Bloomingdales TR 4-2424

ECLECTIC MODERN

By the mid-1950s, reaction to the conformity of the International Style, in addition to an urge to move ahead of the curve, prompted designers to push the boundaries of type—backward. Since the days of William Morris, antique typefaces were used or quoted in contemporary adaptations, yet Modernism's "art of our time" ethos was a decree against pastiche. Modernists fought to end superfluous decoration and ornament, and even rejected the modernistic as a stain on progressive design. Nevertheless, certain designers found that things passé had certain virtues when reprised with intelligence and taste. In response to Late Modern uniformity, New York's Push Pin Studios revived Victorian, Art Nouveau, and Art Deco letterforms not simply to mimic the past, but to enliven the present. This was the beginning of an eclectic rather than dogmatic typography that wed expression and functionality. Push Pin was the foremost proponent, but it was not alone in revisiting and designing its own versions of slab serif Egyptians, Ultra Bodonis, Blackletters, and a range of commercial advertising novelty faces. Eclecticism with a Modern underpinning emerged in the United States

and Europe because mass media demanded more variation, and type, like fashion, constantly renews itself through a process of alternative leaps forward and backward. Type designers from the mid-nineteenth century bastardized the classic letters; likewise in the mid-twentieth century, designers built upon earlier legacies. Returning typography to a period of exuberance, eclecticists advanced the idea that graphic design was both serious and playful. Type did not have to be neutral on a pristine page, nor follow strict guidelines. Eclecticism was a means of giving the written word character and nuance, and this was made increasingly easier because photo typesetting made reviving type economical. The new technology opened the door for more designers (in addition to specialist type designers) to create the occasional one-off face. By reintroducing forgotten letterforms, graphic designers spawned a typographic style rooted in eccentricity.

OPPOSITE: MAHALIA JACKSON, *poster, 1967. Designer: Milton Glaser.*
ABOVE: THE QUICKSILVER MESSENGER SERVICE, *poster, 1966. Designer: Victor Moscoso.*

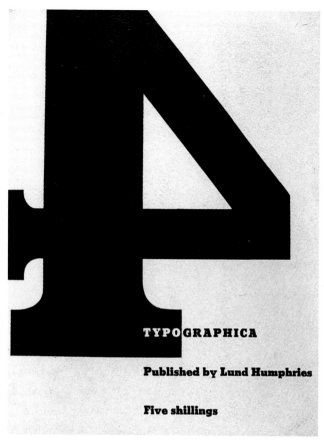

TYPOGRAPHICA

Published by Lund Humphries

Five shillings

410

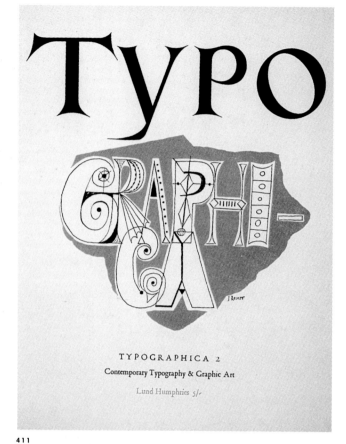

TYPOGRAPHICA 2

Contemporary Typography & Graphic Art

Lund Humphries 5/-

411

This number **6** of ALPHABET AND IMAGE contains copiously illustrated articles on:
(1) 'artistic' Victorian printing   (2) the type designs of Eric Gill

ALPHABET

(3) changes in news presentation in the English provincial press

AND

(4) pre-Raphaelite drawings   (5) architectural drawings by Hugh Casson

IMAGE

Published by ART AND TECHNICS LTD 58 Frith Street, Soho, London W1

Subscription: 7s 6d a copy, or 25s a year post free through your bookseller or direct

412

GBS
ARMS
AND
THE
MAN

THE ARTS THEATRE
6 GREAT NEWPORT STREET WC2

413

P
a new-old type
from
Stephenson Blake

Printed in England

414

ART and
INDUSTRY

35 Cents : November 1940

415

416

ENGLAND

Eclecticism was not simply a historic alternative to International Style Modernism. In England, eclecticism can be traced back to William Morris and the Arts and Crafts movement, the first of the late-nineteenth-century movements to revive historical artifacts as a direct challenge to the monstrosities of industrial-age production. During the early twentieth century, as interest in new typography developed, exemplified in England by Edward Johnston's Railway Type (1916) and Eric Gill's Gill Sans series (1928–30), a counter movement (that included Gill himself) proffered classically inspired typography not so much as a political or philosophical reaction to Modern tendencies, but as a move to retain a semblance of the past amid the onslaught of the new. Yet by the 1940s, many orthodox Modernists combined classical and even nineteenth-century commercial forms, such as slab serif type, for variation in their otherwise austere designs. By the late 1940s and 1950s in England, where fat faces, slab serifs, and Ultra Bodonis were originally popularized, revisiting type of the early consumer age was a trend among designers. Type "culture" journals, notably *Type and Image*, which were devoted to exploring the forgotten histories of type and page design, reintroduced decorative nineteenth-century wood types, for example, as adding visual color and interest in the contemporary context. By the 1950s, graphic design and typography was not constricted to just Modernism or classicism; the confluence of the two resulted in many variations under the banner of eclecticism.

410. TYPOGRAPHICA 4, *periodical cover, 1951. Designer unknown.*

411. TYPOGRAPHICA 2, *periodical cover, 1950. Designer: Imre Reiner.*

412. ALPHABET AND IMAGE, *periodical cover, 1948. Designer unknown.*

413. ARMS AND THE MAN, *advertisement, 1952. Designer unknown.*

414. PLAYBILL, *type specimen, c. 1938. Type designer: Robert Harling.*

415. ART AND INDUSTRY, *periodical cover, 1940. Designer unknown.*

416. NINETEENTH CENTURY ORNAMENTED TYPES AND TITLE PAGES, *book cover, 1954. Designer unknown.*

EUROPE

The destruction of stores of type fonts during World War II took a significant toll on the printing and type founding industries in Europe. If making do with existing supplies of type was the mother of invention, then finding that these curious combinations of old and new had aesthetic virtue and eye-catching appeal determined stylistic variations throughout European countries, where the war had derailed avant-garde Modernist movements. In Germany, Switzerland, and Italy; to a lesser extent Eastern Europe; and eventually even in the USSR, when it began exporting manufactures in the early 1960s, the International Style was widely embraced by corporations doing business in the world market. When it came to more localized publishing and advertising, however, there was less demand to adhere to such conformity. When postwar manufacturing began to create numerous new products and brands, the designer's mission was to find distinctive typography to distinguish and identify products. *Graphis*, Switzerland's most prestigious international graphic design magazine, was the principal promoter of both the International Style and eclecticism, giving credence to the former and legitimacy to the latter. The publication had regular features that showcased designers from different nations, many displaying personal eclectic preferences. These featured designers serving as models and influenced others to sample many typographic options. Eclecticism had a strong footing in Europe, not as dogma, but as a matter-of-fact practice.

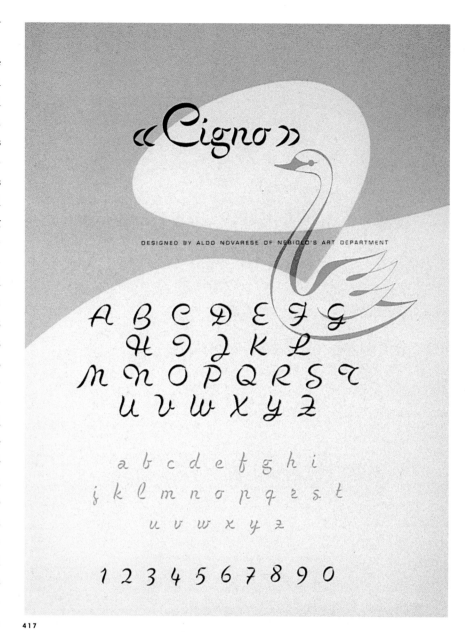

417

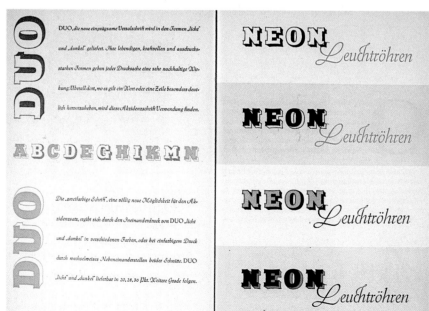

418

419

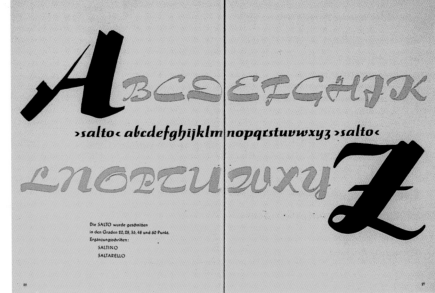

420

421

417. CIGNO, *type specimen, c. 1950.*
Designer: Aldo Novarese.

418. DUO / NEON, *type specimen, 1954.*
Designer: A. Finsterer.

419. NORMANDE, *type specimen, 1954.*
Designer unknown.

420. DIE SALTO, *type specimen, 1954.*
Designer unknown.

421. OPTIK / ORPLID / ROULETTE, *type*
specimen, 1954. Designer: Hans Baum.

UNITED STATES

As critical reaction to the International Style renewed interest in old type styles, it captured the aesthetic interests of young graphic designers. Venerable slab serif faces were never really entirely extinct; indeed, various nineteenth-century typographic materials surfaced in a variety of Modern printed pieces, notably Dada manifestoes. However, the Victoriana pastiche did not emerge as a widespread style until the mid-1950s. Ironically, these artifacts of a bygone age signaled a new, contemporary look for commercial products, particularly records, books, and magazines. Dusting off the old fonts, designers enjoyed mixing and matching the different styles; not in the same manner as their ancestors, who reflexively combined discordant typefaces, but as sophisticates who understood the nuances of type. The results were often charming displays of eccentricity; sometimes they were humorous send-ups of the old style. Some of the alphabets came directly from the original woodtypes, while some were redrawn and put onto film. Connoisseurs of antique woodtypes rose to the increasing demand: Dan X. Solo was the leading archivist and restorer of old type; Rob Roy Kelly chronicled the history; and commercial type shops, such as Morgan Press and Tri-Arts Press, devoted the greater part of their business to revivification.

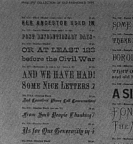

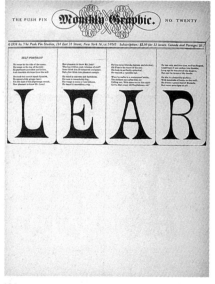

422-423. TRI-ARTS PRESS, *type catalog pages, 1962. Designer unknown.*

424. PUSH PIN MONTHLY GRAPHIC, *periodical cover, 1959. Designer: Seymour Chwast.*

425. MATRIX 7, *periodical cover, 1965. Designers: Hans Barchel / Roger Remington.*

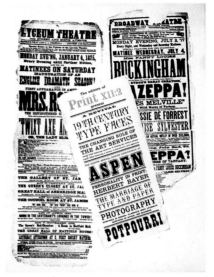

426. MONOCLE, *periodical cover, 1963.*
Designer: Phil Gipps.

427. PRINT XII:2, *periodical cover, 1958.*
Designer: Phil Franznick.

428. MORGAN PRESS, *type catalog cover,*
c. 1965. Designer: John Alcorn.

429

PSYCHEMATS!

Specimen lines on these pages illustrate typical applications of Photo-Lettering's new Psychemat technique. Our Psychemats are designed to sharpen the flavor of the alphabets with which they are used. Their use is not limited to the few styles of letters shown here. The "psm" number next to each line identifies the particular Psychemat design photo-lettered into that line. In theory, this same psyche treatment may be applied to any Photo-Lettering alphabet except styles with fine hairlines. It is our experience that the most striking results are obtained with weights heavier than demibold.

PSYCHEDELITYPES!
PSYCHEDELITYPES!
PSYCHEDELITYPES!
PSYCHEDELITYPES!
PSYCHEDELITYPES!
PSYCHEDELITYPES!
PSYCHEDELITYPES!

430

431

PSYCHEDELITYPES!
PSYCHEDELITYPES
PSYCHEDELITYPES!
PSYCHEDELITYPES
PSYCHEDELITYPES!
PSYCHEDELITYPES!
PSYCHEDELITYPES!
PSYCHEDELITYPES!
PSYCHEDELITYPES!
PSYCHEDELITYPES!!
PSYCHEDELITYPES!
PSYCHEDELITYPES
PSYCHEDELITYPE

432

429. CLEAN-IN, *poster, 1967. Designer: Victor Moscoso.*

430 & 432. PSYCHEDELITYPES, *type specimens (Photo-Lettering Inc.), 1968. Designer unknown.*

431. RITES OF SPRING, *poster, 1967. Designer: Victor Moscoso.*

433

434

PSYCHEDELIA

In the late 1960s, youth culture challenged the values of the previous generation in every sphere of culture, politics, and society. Graphic design reflected the radical shift in attitudes and mores, and psychedelia was the term applied to the new sex, drugs, and rock-and-roll aesthetic that dominated the visual landscape. Psychedelia was on the fringe of the eclectic spectrum, and was devised by self-taught artists who cared little for traditional design and its rules. As Victor Moscoso, one of the leading psychedelic poster artists and the only one to have formal design training, explained, "It was a world turned upside down." Moscoso reversed all the taboos: "The rule that a poster should transmit a message simply and quickly became how long can you engage the viewer in reading the poster? Don't use vibrating colors became use them whenever you can. Lettering should always be legible was changed to make it as difficult as possible to read." Type was scavenged from Victorian bills and Viennese Secessionist posters and printed in fluorescent colors and in raucous compositions. Egyptian faces were given even more exaggerated slab serifs. Psychedelic Playbill was an anomorphic distortion, a commercial wood type drawn entirely in negative space. A nineteenth-century advertising face that gave the appearance of its name, Smoke, was widely used to evoke the ethereal nature of psychedelic art.

433. YOUNGBLOODS, *poster, 1967.*
Designer: Victor Moscoso.

434. BIG BROTHER, *poster, 1967.*
Designer: Victor Moscoso.

UNITED STATES

In America, Late Modernism was fairly individualistic. Nevertheless, a dichotomy developed between those who were influenced by the moderns and those who referenced the past. Every young generation tends to rebel in some way against the preceding generation, and this was obvious during the late 1950s with the emergence of Push Pin Studios as an influence on contemporary graphic design and typography. Push Pin was admittedly an alternative to what its founders, Seymour Chwast and Milton Glaser, described as the cold rigidity of the International Style. As exemplars, if not lynchpins, of American eclecticism, their mission was to revivify old poster traditions, where type and image were seamlessly wed. In doing so, they revisited the emblematic typefaces of Victorian, Art Nouveau, and Art Deco eras, and used them for display and to complement their period-inspired graphics. Push Pin did not, however, simply make pastiche, but rather invented new forms based on these influences. Chwast's interest in Art Nouveau and *Jugendstil* resulted in his design of Artone, a proprietary typeface for an ink company that combined curvilinear and slab serif forms. Milton Glaser's curiosity in quirky novelty faces of the 1930s inspired Baby Teeth, a blocky stair-step typeface that referred to the past but was also emblematic of the present. During the late 1950s, and with the advent of phototypesetting in the 1960s, revivalism took root. Old wood and hot-metal typefaces were resurrected from lost typecases and hellboxes and became a dominant editorial and advertising style.

RINGLET ringlet
ABCDEFGHIJKLMNOPQRSTUVWXYZ? abcdefghijklmnopqrstuvwxyz%$¢2357

ROBUST robust
ABCDEFGHIJKLMNOPQRSTUVWXYZabcdefghijklmnopqrstuvwxyz2357

ROMAN no. 1
ABCDEFGHIJKLMNOPQRSTUVWXYZ?&¢abcdefghijklmnopqrstuvwxyz%$¢2357

ROMAN NO. 1 outline

ROMAN ornate
ABC DEFGHIJKLMNOPQRST UVWXYZ&?2357abcdefghijklmnopqrstuvwxyz

ROYAL ornate
ABCDEF GHIJKLMNOPQRSTUVWXYZ?&%abcdefghijklmnopqrstuvwxyz%$¢3579

RUBENS Extended
ABCDEFGHIJKLMNOPQRSTUVWXYZ?&abcdefghijklmnopqrstuvwxyz$¢2468

RUBENS Ex. cond.
ABCDEFGHIJKLMNOPQRSTUVWXYZ&?2357abcdefghijklmnopqrstuvwxyz

SANDS sands
ABCDEFGHIJKLMNOPQRSTUVWXYZ?&abcdefghijklmnopqrstuvwxyz$¢2367

SCHAFT schaft
ABCDEF GHIJKLMNOPQRSTUVWX YZ?&abcdefghijklmnopqrstuvwxyz$¢2357

SEA CROW CAPS
ABCDEFGHIJKLMNOPQRSTUVWXYZ

SEVEN STAR seven star
ABCDEFGHIJKLMNOPQRSTUVWXYZ&?abcdefghijklmnopqrstuvwxyz$¢2357

seig seig
ABCDEFGHIJKLMNOPQRSTU VWXYZ&?2357abcdefghijklmnopqrstuvwxyz

SKIDOO CAPS
ABCDEFGHIJKLMNOPQRSTUVWXYZ?&$¢2357

435

435. RINGLET, ET AL., *font, type specimens (various ornate types), 1968. Design director: Martin Solomon.*

436. ARTONE, *alphabet, 1968. Type designer: Seymour Chwast.*

437. HOLOGRAM, *alphabet, 1970. Type designer: Milton Glaser.*

438. BABY TEETH, *alphabet, 1968. Type designer: Milton Glaser.*

439. GLASER STENCIL, *alphabet, 1970. Type designer: Milton Glaser.*

440. FILM SENSE, *alphabet, 1969. Type designer: Seymour Chwast.*

441. BLIMP, *alphabet, 1970. Type designer: Seymour Chwast.*

ABCDEFGHI
JKLMNOPQR
abcdefghijk
436

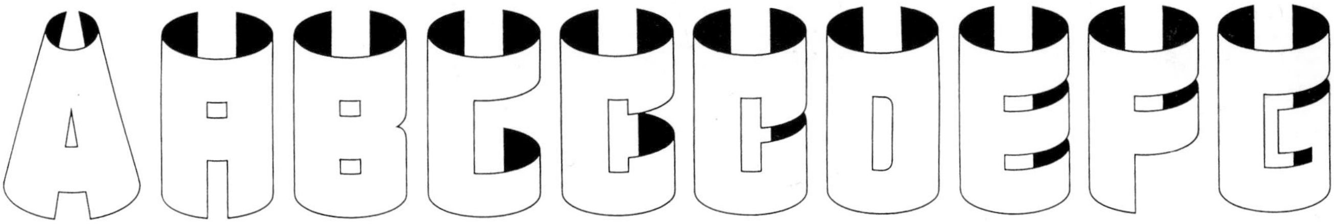

AABBCCCDEFG
437

ABCDEFGHI
ABCDEFGHI
438

ABC ABC ABC
439 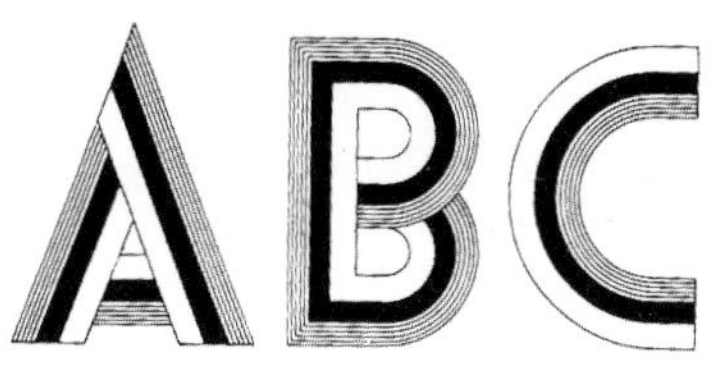   440 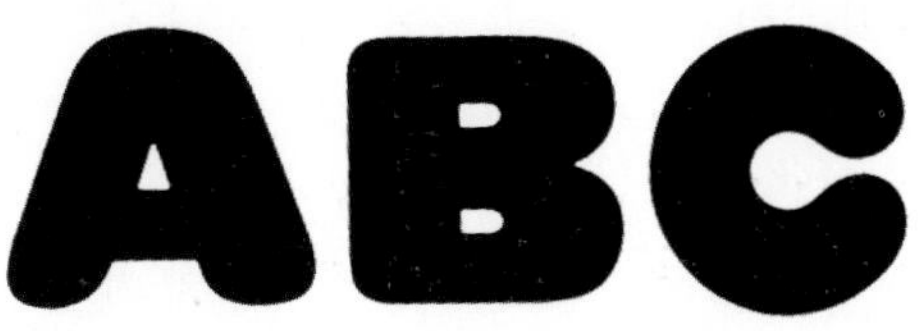   441

165

OPEN HERE

LETTERROR

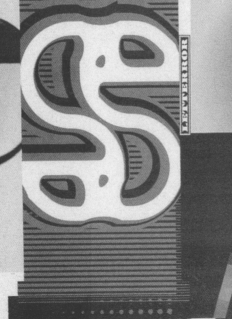
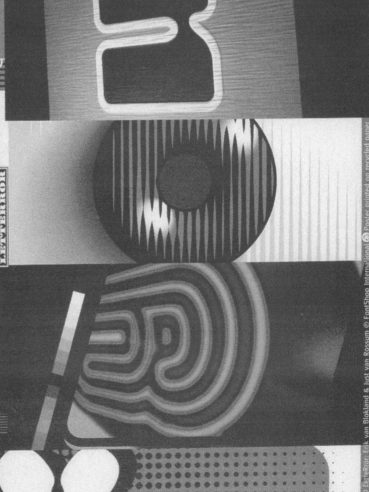

FF WhatYouSee © LetterError: Erik van Blokland & Just van Rossum © FontShop International ♻ Poster printed on recycled paper

P O S T M O D E R N

Eclectic Modern was Postmodern before the term was officially coined and before so-called "Eurocentric" Modernism fell into the sinkhole of 1980s political correctness. As it refers to graphic and type design, Postmodern is a broad rubric that includes a wide range of aesthetic and formal concerns on one hand, and generational issues on the other (as in passing the baton from one generation to the next, and from one time-honored approach to a new one). Postmodern means busting the rules established by the previous generation. Postmodern is the argument for diversity (or eclecticism) in form and style. Postmodern is the celebration of individuality, rather than a universal design language. Post-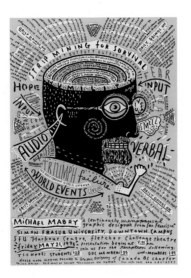modern is rooted in the computer revolution and the burgeoning of digital type design. Postmodern is the integration of theory, politics, and social relations into the look and feel of design. Postmodern is ultimately a simple term used to pigeonhole a wide range of prac-tice during the 1980s and 1990s, at which time the graphic design profession underwent a meteoric rise and type (fonts) became both less arcane and more integrated into the general life of the masses. Many subcategories of stylistic and formal activity exist under the umbrella—New Wave, Grunge, Deconstruction—each with common traits. Complexity replaced simplicity, subjectivity replaced objectivity, and ornament returned. The digital revolution, like the shift from hot metal to phototype before it, demanded the remaking of existing typefaces. Yet this paradigm shift also encouraged increased experimentation. The challenge for those designers working with the new media was to respect convention while extending the boundaries of existing design. Since type styles have always been closely linked to current technology, there was no reason not to design type that represented the computer age. By the late 1980s, Emigre Fonts explored low-resolution design; by the early 1990s, high-resolution fontography further opened the floodgates for many more precisionist custom faces and outrageous novelties than in perhaps all the other typographic eras combined.

OPPOSITE: WHATYOUSEE, *poster for FUSE, 1995. Designers: Erik van Blockland and Just van Rossum.*
ABOVE: STRIP MINING FOR SURVIVAL, *poster, 1993. Designer: Michael Mabry.*

SWITZERLAND

From the land of functional graphic design came the next revolution in type. Rosmarie Tissi and Siegfried Odermatt departed from traditional Swiss formats, but Wolfgang Weingart, a former student at Gewerbeschule in Basel, was the first to unhinge type from the bolts of the grid. He once wrote that, in Switzerland, "One direction is the well-known, moderate-objective or rational direction . . . Another direction is a newer tendency toward a lively, relatively free kind of typography which renounces extensive design dogma . . . But this second is unthinkable without the classical 'Swiss Typography,' in that it is a logical further development of it." Weingart eliminated indents at the beginning of paragraphs, changed type weights in mid-word, and increased and decreased letterspacing in the same sentence. From the late 1960s to mid-1970s, Weingart challenged the constraints of hot-metal type. Afterward, he immersed himself in photoreproduction. He became obsessed with enlarged halftone dots, the illusion of movement, and layers of meaning. He took previously taboo notions of gridlocked composition and expanded the parameters of the page. As a typography teacher, Weingart encouraged students to invoke wit, as well as alternative type patterns, and his accolytes spread his typographic diversity into the world.

442. STRAUHOF, *poster, 1981. Designers: Odermatt and Tissi.*

443. TYPOGRAFICHE MONATSBLÄTTER, *periodical cover, 1983. Designers: Odermatt and Tissi.*

444. HERBERT BAYER, *poster, 1982. Designer: Wolfgang Weingart.*

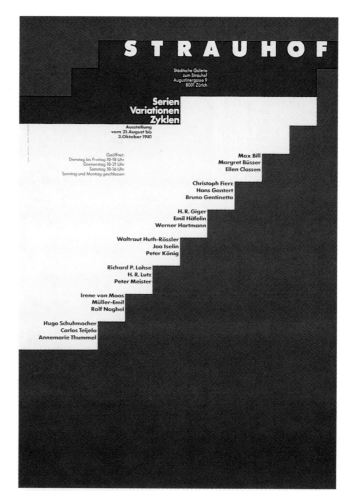

442

443

Herbert **Bayer**
Das künstlerische Werk
1918–1938

GEWERBE
MUSEUM
BASEL

2. Juli–29. August 1982

ТЕОРИЯ. ПРАКТИКА

Иллюстрированный научно-практический журнал. Министерство торговли СССР. Межведомственный совет по рекламе. Основан в марте 1971 г. Выходит 6 раз в год. РЕКЛАМА. Мос

В НОМЕРЕ

клуб потребителей	1	ИНДЕКС ДОВЕРИЯ Ю. ХАЧАТУРОВ, Л. БОЧИН
ваше мнение?	3	УЧАСТВУЕМ В ПОЛИТИКЕ Н. СМИРНОВА
городская среда	5	ВОЗВРАЩЕНИЕ НЕОНА
деловым людям	8	«СВОБОДНЫХ МЕСТ...» — ЕСТЬ Л. ОЧЕРЕТ
на страницах и экранах	9	ЗА СЛОВОМ — В КАРМАН! О. ЗУБКОВА
дизайн и мы	12	АВАНГАРДНАЯ КЛАССИКА Г. КУРЬЕРОВА
деловым людям	16	«ИНТЕРКВАДРО»: ОТ ПРОЕКТА ДО ВНЕДРЕНИЯ И. КРУГЛОВА
хроника	17	С ХЛЕБОМ-СОЛЬЮ — В БЕЛЫЙ ДОМ И. ЛЕБЕДЕВА
в четыре краски	18	И СНОВА ПОЛЬСКИЙ ПЛАКАТ В. ЦЫГАНКОВ
организация рекламы	20	ФОРМИРОВАНИЕ СПРОСА В ФИРМЕННЫХ МАГАЗИНАХ Е. ПУШКИНА
вам в помощь	23	ОБ ОПЛАТЕ ТРУДА ВНЕШТАТНЫХ ХУДОЖНИКОВ И ФОТОГРАФОВ

главный редактор
И. БОРЗЕНКОВ

редакционная коллегия
В. АКОПОВ
Е. АСС
А. ГАМОВ
В. ГЛАЗУНОВА
Е. КАНЕВСКИЙ
В. КИСЕЛЕВ
зам. гл. редактора
А. ЛЕЙКИНА
Б. ЛЕНСКИЙ
Н. ОЛЕЙНИКОВ
А. ОРЛОВ
А. СЕМЕНКОВ
отв. секретарь
Н. СМИРНОВА
И. РОЖКОВ
Н. РОМАНЕНКО
И. ТЕР-АРАКЕЛЯН
Ю. ХАЧАТУРОВ
В. ХОЛОДОВ
редактор отдела
В. ЦЫГАНКОВ
Ю. ЧЕРНЯХОВСКИЙ

редакторы
О. ЗУБКОВА
О. ПЕКУРОВСКАЯ

художественно-
технический редактор
Б. ЗЕЛЬМАНОВИЧ

консультант по вопросам
визуальной рекламы
искусствовед
С. СЕРОВ

проект оформления
В. ЧАЙКА
А. ГЕЛЬМАН (1-я стр. обл.)
В. ЦЫГАНКОВ
(макет и фото)
В. ЕФИМОВ, А. ТАРБЕЕВ
(оформление 4-й стр. обл.)
В. РАЙТМАН (фото)

Сдано в набор 15.09.89
Подписано
в печать 14.11.89
А—13124
Печать офсетная
Бумага Корюковка ДЧ 120 г
Формат $60 \times 90^{1}/_{8}$
Усл. печ. л. 3,0.
Уч.-изд. л. 5,2
Объем в усл. кр.-отт. 816,0
Тираж 68 000 экз.
Заказ 5436. Цена 70 коп.
Адрес редакции: 103062
Москва
ул. Чернышевского, 45-5-32
тел. 227-02-92
Московская
типография № 5
Государственного
комитета СССР
по печати
129243 Москва
Мало-Московская ул., 21

© Реклама. 1989

445
170

446

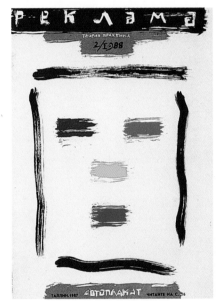

447

448

449

450

RUSSIA

In the early 1960s, the United States Information Agency sent two exhibitions, *Architecture U.S.A.* and *Design U.S.A.*, to Russia and exposed Russian designers to the Swiss style and Helvetica (a Cyrillic version was cut for Russia). By the early 1970s, the Union of Trade Advertising was founded, which published a magazine called *Reklame* to survey the work of advertising design groups throughout the Soviet Union. The Swiss magazine *Graphis* was also passed around like samizdat publications. By 1984, when the words *glasnost, perestroika* and *demokratia* were announced to the world, a new graphic excitement emerged in the Baltic Republics of Latvia, Estonia, and Lithuania. That year, Latvian artist Laimonis Chenberg, of Riga, exhibited a poster called "Perestroika?" that signaled the first time that official policy was lampooned with irony and wit. It triggered a chain reaction that influenced Muscovite designers almost immediately. It also launched a new graphic style based more on Polish poster traditions and avant-garde typography than the Socialist Realism of the past. The most unusual examples of this "new wave" were covers of the late 1980s issues of *Reklama* that revealed interest in a range of typographic styles. Consistent with new waves in the West, type exploded off the pages.

---

445. REKLAME, *table of contents, 1990. Art Director: Zelmanovitz.*

446. EVOLUTION?, *poster, 1988. Designer unknown.*

447-450. REKLAME (ADVERTISING), *periodical covers, 1987–90. Designers unknown.*

ENGLAND

The digital revolution democratized type design and opened the discipline to include not only the professional type designer, but graphic designers who design type. The English contribution to digital type has been immense. From historical revival to raucous experimentation, English type designers, including Phil Baines, Neville Brody, and Jonathan Barnbrook; design magazines such as *Eye, Fuse,* and *Octavo*; and type conferences like Type90 and FUSE, have pushed the form and application of type into realms that stretch once-sacrosanct standards. Besides the utilitarian, many English typefaces have symbolic and philosophical implications that extend beyond the traditional function of type as a vessel of meaning. Perhaps the most controversial aspect of English type design is the experimental movement that blurs legibility and readability, resulting in symbolic marks that serve as codes for ideas. Through *Fuse,* the digital type "magazine" edited by Brody and Jon Wozencroft (who called it "a dynamic new forum for typography") and published by FontShop, an international array of experimentalists have introduced alphabets that have altered perception of the form. Some are representational/traditional while others are incomprehensibly abstract. The themes of each number of *Fuse,* which contributors are requested to address in type they have designed, transcend common type concerns and include larger issues of politics and culture (i.e. pornography and London traffic). The result is a liberating use of unconventional types to interpret these issues.

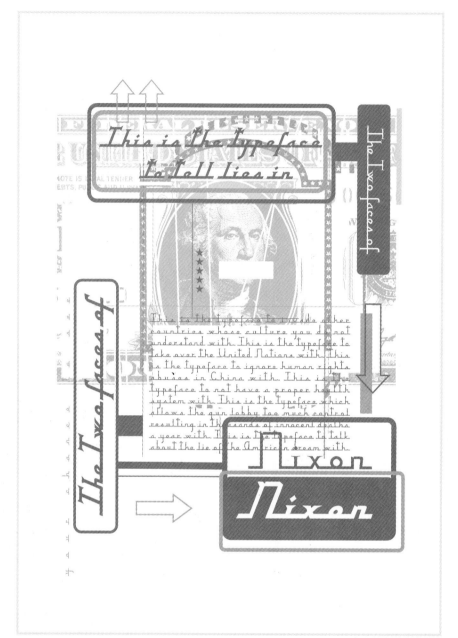

451

451. NIXON, *type specimen, 1998. Designer: Jonathan Barnbrook.*

452-453. OCTAVO, *periodical cover and inside spread, 1988–90. Designer: Hamish Muir / 8vo.*

454. FUSE 10 (FREEFORM), *type specimen poster, 1994. Designer: Neville Brody.*

455. FUSE 11 (PEEP), *type specimen poster, 1994. Designer: Neville Brody.*

452

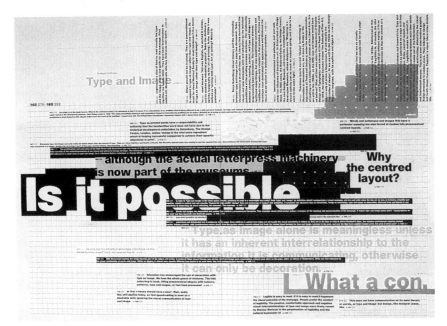

453

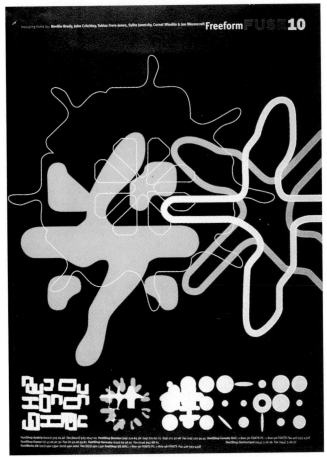

454

455

UNITED STATES VERNACULAR

In linguistic terms, *vernacular* suggests a common vocabulary, that, over time, is understood by all members of a group or culture. In graphic design terms, it is that indigenous commercial art that may have been professionally or naively produced and is a shared component of the broad visual landscape, like a barbershop sign or a Good Humor ice cream logo. Interest in the vernacular has always been present in graphic design; in the 1950s, for example, designers were smitten with primitive signs and, of course, the old woodtypes that were part of them. In the mid-1980s, yet another revivification of the past entered sophisticated design precincts, starting in architecture and invading graphic design. One facet was the reprise of 1920s and 1930s commercial printer's stock clichés used on matchbooks and advertisements, as practiced by Charles Spencer Anderson and the Duffy Group. Another was the reappreciation of passé design styles, described as "retro," such as Paula Scher's adaptation of Constructivism. Another was M&Co.'s interest in the visual detritus of mass culture. Through the personal and house styles of each of these designers and firms, historical artifacts both high and low were recast as contemporary design attributes.

456. CROSS COUNTRY DESIGN TOUR, *poster, 1994. Designer: Charles Spencer Anderson.*

457. AMERICAN CENTER FOR DESIGN, *catalog cover, 1994. Designer: Charles Spencer Anderson.*

458. BLADE TO THE HEAT, *poster, 1997. Designer: Paula Scher.*

456

457

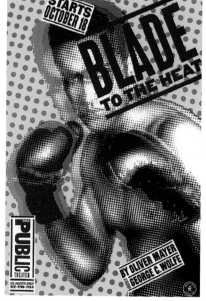

458

459

460

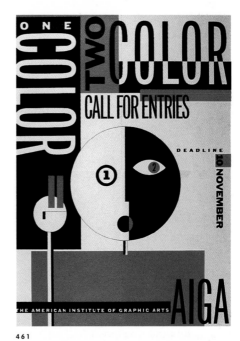

461

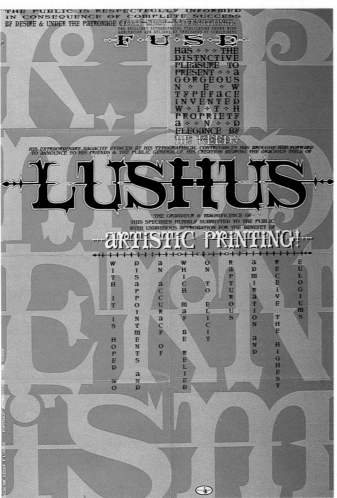

462

463

---

459. JODY'S DINING HALL, *poster, 1998.*
Designer: Yee-Haw.

460. HOT IDEAS, *poster, 1992. Designer:*
John Sayles.

461. ONE COLOR TWO COLOR, *poster,*
1992. Designer: Michael Mabry.

462. LUSHUS. *FUSE poster, 1992.*
Designer: Jeffery Keedy.

463. PROVERBS 25:11, *brochure*
page for Audible Inc., 1997. Designer:
Funny Garbage.

464

465

466

467

468

469

470

464. W E T, *periodical cover, 1980. Designer unknown.*

465. F E T I S H, *periodical cover, 1984. Designers: David Sterling and Jane Kosstrin.*

466. A I G A, *poster, 1988. Designers: Pat and Greg Samata.*

467. C A N T O N M A R K E T, *alphabet, 1995. Type designer: Daniel Pelavin.*

468. T E S T, *alphabet, 1996. Type designer: Daniel Pelavin.*

469-470. W O R K S P I R I T : V I T R A D E S I G N J O U R N A L, *periodical pages, 1988. Designer: April Greiman.*

U N I T E D S T A T E S N E W W A V E

The New Wave first hit the shores of the United States in the early 1980s, a confluence of European punk and Swiss new wave that evolved from an experimental method into a commercial mannerism. The initial appearance of work in the United States by Basel-educated, American-born April Greiman was a departure from the 1970s Late Modern sensibilities. While eclectic typography had dominated, it was a mixture of nostalgic imagery and swashful type. The bold sans serif Univers type used in a publication designed by Greiman titled *WorkSpirit*, for example, juxtaposed light and heavy weights with heavy rules, extreme leading, and wide letterspacing layered over brightly colored images; it indicated a distinct break from the dominant style and was precursor of a new typographic aesthetic. She was one of the foremost interpreters of the Weingart approach, though not a carbon copy. In early 1982, Greiman had early access to state-of-the-art video and digitizing equipment, and with Jayme Odgers, she began integrating photomontage and type in posters and brochures that had a futuristic evocation. The Macintosh computer was introduced in 1984, and by 1986 Greiman pioneered the marriage of text to digitized video images. Where new wave ends, if at all, is subject to debate. By the early 1990s, many of the ideas that Greiman promoted were incorporated into other innovations and derivations by scores of young designers. Disruption of conventional reading pathways and new expressive typefaces contributed to the air of rebelliousness.

UNITED STATES
DECONSTRUCTION

In 1914, F. T. Marinetti announced, "My revolution is aimed at the so-called typographical harmony of the page, which is contrary to the flux and reflux, the leaps and bursts of style that run through the page. On the same page, therefore, we will use three or four colors of ink, or even twenty different typefaces if necessary." The relevance of this statement seventy years hence is evidenced by current type styles that frolic in clutter. These styles, which owe a spiritual debt to the pioneer Modernists, have come to define this age symbolically as definitively as the Swiss grid did for an earlier generation. There are many ways to categorize the typographic machinations of the present. One such approach, under the rubric Deconstruction, is a scholarly method of analyzing "texts" (introduced by Poststructuralist critic Jacques Derrida) that asks the receiver of visual and textual message to comprehend the complexity of meaning. During the late 1980s, graphic design graduate students at the Cranbrook Academy in Michigan adapted Deconstruction theory as a means to design printed material. The translation of this theory as graphic design involved complex typographic compositions in which formula and equilibrium are disrupted and form and content are forced into interpretive relationships.

471. FLUXUS, *poster, 1989. Designer: Katherine McCoy.*

472. MY BEACH, *periodical pages (Beach Culture), 1990. Designer: David Carson.*

473-475. CAMPBELLS LABEL SERIES, *student project, 1984. Designer: Jeffery Keedy.*

471

472

473

474

475

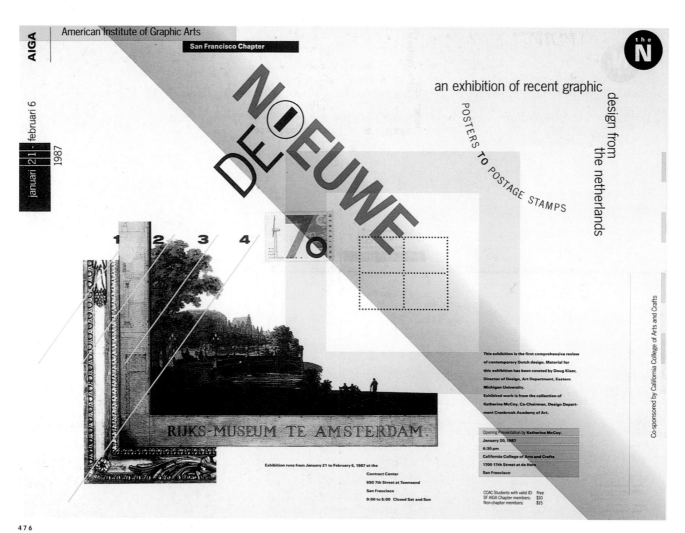

476

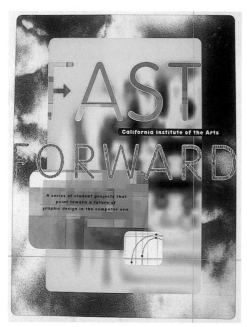

477

478

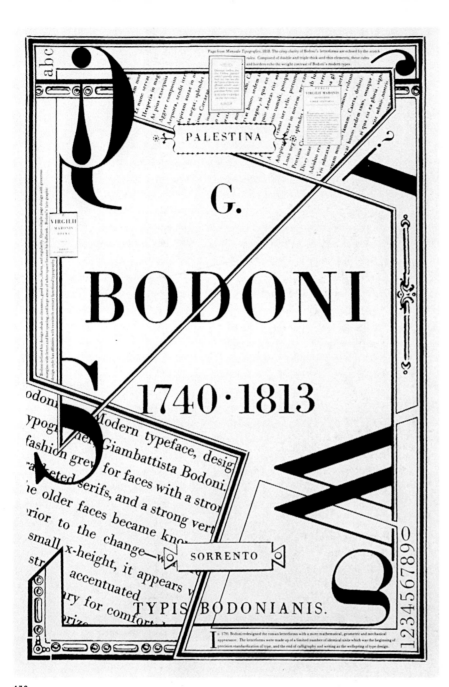

479

The overlay of intellectual theory on both rational and intuitive processes has been highly criticized as an excuse for cluttered design that obscures meaning. Even some of the proponents of Deconstruction, including former Cranbrook design chair Katherine McCoy, argue that some of these are ideas are better suited to art than to client-driven messages. Yet the principles on which Deconstruction is based are applicable, if not useful, to conveying a certain kind of message in an information-saturated, digitally linked society. The hierarchies inherent in the multiple layers of written information force readers to scan in bites, rather than in linear fashion. The linear narrative, it is argued, is not the only way to navigate text. For those who can decode the structure, comprehension is fairly easy. The students who accepted the fundamental premise that meaning is complex and therefore typography should express multiple options were seeking appropriate ways to project their own design codes. For some, Deconstruction was a means to see the printed page (or screen) anew; for others, it was yet another style. Layering and distortion are characteristics of typography that is designed to emote and to be read.

---

476. DE NIEUWE, *poster, 1988. Designer: Lucille Tenazas.*

477. FAST FOWARD, *CalArts catalog cover, 1996. Designer: James Stoecker.*

478. LIVING SURFACES, *ACD conference announcement, 1993. Designer: P. Scott Makela.*

479. G.BODONI, *poster, 1984. Designer: Jeffery Keedy.*

UNITED STATES
EMIGRE

In 1983, a year before the introduction of the Macintosh computer, Rudy VanderLans and Zuzana Licko founded a culture magazine called *Emigre*; within a few years it changed focus and developed into the clarion of digital typography and design. The first Macintosh and its bit-mapped default faces inspired *Emigre*'s founders to design original typefaces for their magazine specifically and the computer environment in general. They founded a type business, Emigre Graphics (later called Emigre Fonts); one of the earliest digital foundries, it became a pioneer in unconventional typeface design, introducing innovative dot-matrix (Bitmap Oblique, Oakland Six) and high-resolution digital typefaces (Modula Serif, Democratica Bold). *Emigre* magazine further showcased other leading practitioners of the new typography and sold their experiments in the practical arena. *Emigre* became a touchstone for progress, but the paradox is that it also provided templates for mimicry. What *Emigre* initiated was co-opted by the new mainstream, from fashion magazines to MTV. *Emigre* was not just the standard bearer, but the bearer of standards for experimental digital typography. When other serious type designers adapted traditional methods to the digital medium, *Emigre* created a uniquely digital environment. While launching a business, VanderLans and Licko took courageous leaps in the selection of faces they represented and the ones they designed. Not content to follow tradition, they created a tradition of their own.

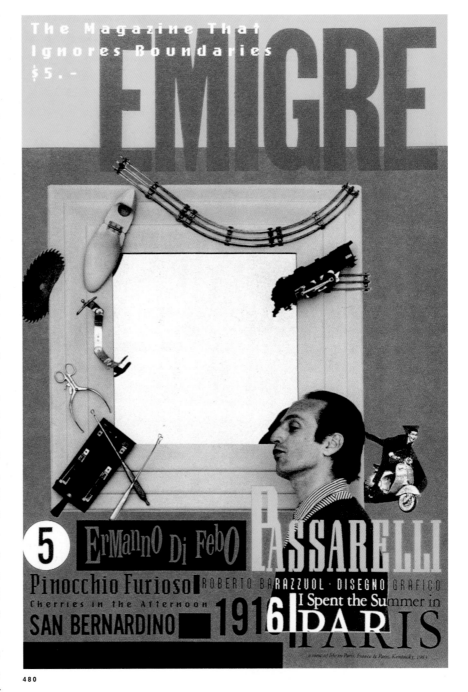

480

480. EMIGRE NO. 5, *periodical cover, 1986. Designers: Rudy VanderLans and Zuzana Licko / Emigre Graphics.*

481. OUTWEST, *type specimen, 1993. Type designer: Ed Fella. Poster designer: Rudy VanderLans / Emigre Graphics.*

482. DOGMA, *type specimen, 1994. Type designer: Zuzana Licko / Emigre Graphics.*

483. EMIGRE NO. 19, *periodical cover, 1995. Designer: Rudy VanderLans / Emigre Graphics.*

484. TEMPLATE GOTHIC, *type specimen, 1991. Type designer: Barry Deck / Emigre Graphics.*

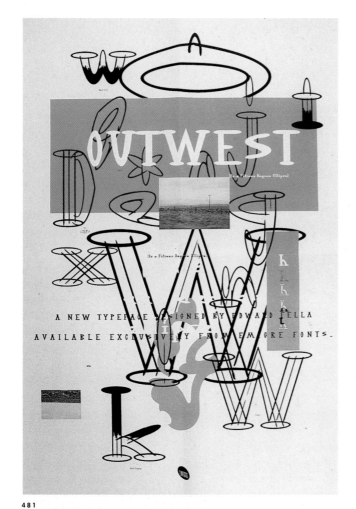

481

Dogma Extra Outline, Dogma Outline · $59

ABCDEFGHIJKLMNOPQRSTUVWXYZ1234567
890abcdefghijklmnopqrstuvwxyz

ABCDEFGHIJKLMNOPQRSTUVWXYZ1234567890
abcdefghijklmnopqrstuvwxyz

Dogma Bold, Dogma Black, Dogma Script Bold · $95

ABCDEFGHIJKLMNOPQRSTUVWXYZ12345678
90abcdefghijklmnopqrstuvwxyz

ABCDEFGHIJKLMNOPQRSTUVWXYZ123
4567890abcdefghijklmnopqrstuvwxyz

ABCDEFGHIJKLMNOPQRSTUVWXYZ12345
67890abcdefghijklmnopqrstuvwxyz

482

483

A a B b C c D d E e F f G g H i
J j K k L l M m N n O o P p Q q
R r S s T t U u V v W w X x Y y Z z

A a B b C c D d E e F f G g H i
J j K k L l M m N n O o P p Q q
R r S s T t U u V v W w X x Y y Z z

484

485

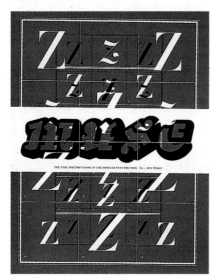

486

487

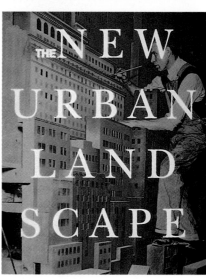

488

485. EX LIBRIS, *Champion Paper promotion, 1996. Designer: Stephen Doyle.*

486. MUSE, *type catalog cover (Hoefler Type Foundry), 1997. Designer: Jonathan Hoefler.*

487. HTF HOEFLER TEX, *type specimen (Hoefler Type Foundry), 1997. Type designer: Jonathan Hoefler.*

488. NEW URBAN LANDSCAPE, *book-cover, 1988. Designer: Stephen Doyle.*

489

490

UNITED STATES NEW CLASSICISM

Phototype was never perfect enough to recreate the nuances of many great metal typefaces. Digital media simplifies the process and allows for greater variations within type families. The numerous current digital foundries accessible through the internet have, in turn, designed hundreds of new fonts for the marketplace. The digital revolution spawned many eccentric display typefaces, but perhaps among the most enduring will be the classical and other historical revivals used for body text and headlines. The history of type is in part rooted in the quest to perfect the great types of previous ages, and so like those who make digital remasters of classical music, type designers such as Jonathan Hoefler and Tobias Frere-Jones have given new life to old faces like Bodoni and Baskerville. They have also developed new faces based on these classical materials, but added those nuances and attributes that they lacked when current. Many of these faces are created for publishing, advertising, and computer clients who desire exclusive, proprietary alphabets. Like the king of France in the seventeenth century, these companies are patrons of an iconoclastic breed of type designer. The New Classicism is about both revival and invention, because there is no sense in remaking type that has existed before without improving upon it.

489. DIDOT, *type specimen poster (Hoefler Type Foundry), 1996. Type designer: Jonathan Hoefler.*

490. NOT CASLON, *type specimen poster (Emigre Fonts), 1996. Type designer: Mark Andersen.*

UNITED STATES GRUNGE

The term *grunge* signifies hard-rocking, post-Punk music that originated in Seattle and suggests the untidy appearance of its adherents. As type, the rubric indicates the grungy or distressed appearance of typefaces that shake, shimmy, and shiver; that are distressed and decayed; and in most instances that look like they were scrawled in dirt rather than cut in stone. The grunge "style" emerged out of the computer era and the desktop publishing phenomenon. It could never have occurred when type design was the sole provenance of professional type designers. With Fontographer software, however, the individualistic, expressionistic, and narcissistic urges allow designers to create any and all kinds of letter-forms. David Carson was the most adventuresome of the grunge designers, and through his early experimentation with the Macintosh, he developed a typographic vocabulary and style that turned taboos into virtues. With the advent of digital type foundries like T-26, Garage-Fonts, and Plazm Fonts, which license designs from professionals and novices alike, the market embraced typographic visionaries and eccentrics who produce expressionistic type as art and satire.

491. VISCOSITY REGULAR AND INLINE, *alphabet (FontBoy), 1996. Type designers: Bob Aufuldish & Kathy Warriner.*

492. ROARSHOCK, *1996–1967. Type designers: Bob Aufuldish & Kathy Warriner.*

493. KGB, *periodical cover, 1996. Designers: Nancy Mazzi & Brian Kelly.*

494. JESUS SAVES, *type specimen, 1996. Designer: Paul Sych / Thirstype.*

495. RAW, *periodical cover, 1985. Designers: Art Spiegelman, Françoise Mouly.*

491

492

493

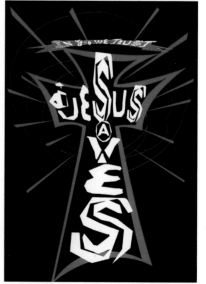

494

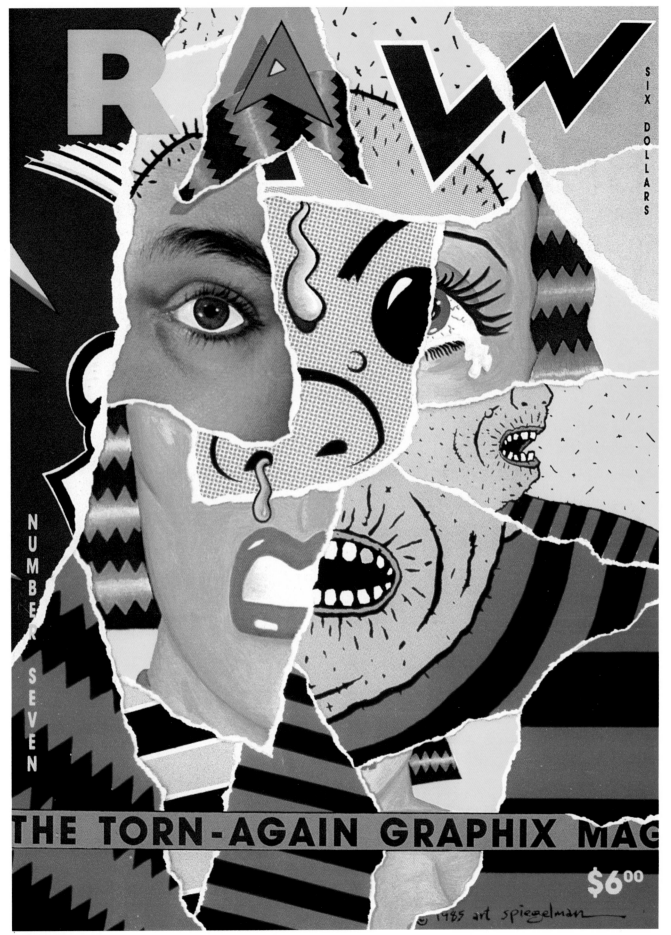

495

ABCNEᵣCIII
JKLᴧINOPQ
RSTUⱱWXYZ
496

ABCDEFGHIJ
KLMNOPQR
STUVWXYZ
497

ABCDEFGHI
JKLMNOPQR
STUVWXYZ
498

abcdefghijklm
nopqrstuvwxyz
499

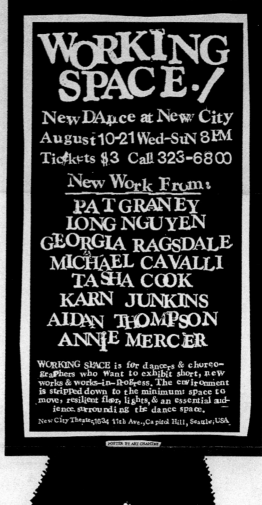

500

ABCDEFGHIJKLM
NOPQRSTUVWX
YZ123456789
abcdefghijklm
nopqrstuvwxyz!

501

502

503

UNITED STATES GRUNGE

"Against the backdrop of defaults and prepackaged templates," wrote type designer Tobias Frere-Jones (*Zed*, 1994), "grunge stands as a rebellion against the default of the computer." The intial attempts to progress beyond the constraints of this medium opened the floodgates for scores of talented and less-than-talented designers to create an untold number individualistic fonts. Admittedly the computer is the most powerful tool that graphic designers possess, but it is also the progenitor of mediocrity. Despite its remarkable memory and random access, the computer houses tried and true standards of status quo design. Like the International Style, the right angle is its god, the grid is its totem. Left in the hands of conventional designers, it is programmed to act as an assembly line, churning out perfect specimens of conformity. For those who use it as a desktop publishing tool, it does its job flawlessly; but for the iconoclastic type designer the computer's perfection is its fatal flaw. Conversely, building errors onto the hard drive makes the computer a bit, well, more human. The grunge typographer is ostensibly teasing the computer, making a virtue of its mistakes. Like tempting the goody-two-shoes or little-miss-perfect to do naughty acts, grunge makes the machine perform counter to its programming; by using digital detritus and visual noise to affect a typographic anomaly, grunge type degrades notions of purity as it guffaws in the face of conformity. Grunge may not survive beyond this short epoch, but it will leave behind the sense that type is mutable.

496. CHAIN LETTER, *type specimens, 1995. Designer: Tobias Frere-Jones.*

497. GRUNGE, *alphabet, 1995. Designer: Scott Yoshinga / Plazm Fonts.*

498. M.K. ULTRA, *alphabet, 1995. Designer: Mike Bain / GarageFonts.*

499. SUCUBUS EVIL, *alphabet, 1996. Designer: Mark Clifton, based on writing by Amanda Lewis / GarageFonts.*

500. NEW CITY THEATER, *poster (with transfer type), 1990. Designer: Art Chantry.*

501. CONECTADODOTS, *alphabet, 1997. Designer: Gustavo E. Ugarte / GarageFonts.*

502. T-26, *catalog cover, 1995. Designer: Klassen.*

503. SIDEWALKER, *type specimen, 1995. Type designer: Schiavi Fabrizio / T-26.*

504

505

506

507

508

509

510

511

512

EXPERIMENTAL

An experiment is a viable way to test the tolerance of a typeface in real world, but a typeface designed to be experimental as an end in itself suggests a lack of confidence in its utility. Type designer Jonathan Hoefler says that the term *experimental* tends to be an alibi for not addressing flaws: "It becomes a way of closing off discussion." He prefers the term *speculative*, for when a designer speculates on a new design the process of trial and error kicks in immediately. Experimental can be a euphemism for "unusual." Indeed, most of the typefaces so dubbed are mildly or radically unusual, but there is virtue to experimentation. Not all type is designed for public consumption; rather some is created as a formal exercise that may be to be used once or twice on a personal project. Elliott Earls and Michael Worthington design and then play (read experiment) with type long before they release it to the world. Nevertheless, much so-called experimentation today appears on the public stage simply because it exists; distributed over the Internet, it may find its way to designers hungry for hipness. Some experimental typefaces are designed simply to foster debate over the efficacy of such work.

504–508. DIGITAL EXPERIENCE, *video titles, 1998. Designer: Michael Worthington.*

509. PLAZM, *periodical cover, 1998. Art director: Josh Berger. Designer: Ed Fella.*

510. FETISH NOS. 126, 338, 976, *type specimen, 1996–98. Type designer: Jonathan Hoefler.*

511. ELLIOTT, *performance poster, 1998. Designer: Elliott Earls.*

512. MAU, *poster, 1997. Designer: Elliott Earls.*

LATER MODERN

Although still practiced by loyal adherents, Modernism devolved into a mannerism without a mission—a surface without a soul. Since it is axiomatic that every action fosters a reaction, the Postmodern reaction is ready for its own challengers. Does this mean that a return to Avant-Garde, Commercial, or Late Modernism is on the horizon? For some designers a "less is more" aesthetic—a confluence of modernist and classicist sensibilities —emerges as a viable response to the fashionable clutter of the past decade. Modernism will probably not return in the pure form that its founding masters practiced it. The essence of healthy art, graphic design, and typography is to build on the past, not to revert to it. Even the recent retro pastiche periods evolved from nostalgia into some kind of currency. Later Modernism is an appropriate way to describe typography that does not fit neatly into the various Postmodern camps, yet is also not slavishly following antiquated Modern traditions. Later Modern is a continuation, a search for formal discipline, moral center, and invention. It is not beholden to contemporary style and fashion instead the designers of this genre create it.

513

514

515

516

513. "WHAT IS AIDS?", *periodical pages (Colors), 1995. Editor: Tibor Kalman.*

514. MECHANISM, *Columbus Society of Communication Arts newsletter, 1995. Crit Warren / Schmeltz & Warren.*

515. KURT WEIL, *album cover, 1985. Designers: Tibor Kalman and Alex Isley.*

516. (NOTHING BUT) FLOWERS, *Talking Heads music video, 1988. Designer: Tibor Kalman with Emily Oberman / M&Co.*

517. DESIGN MILWAUKEE, *poster, 1993. Designer: Planet Design Company.*

design Milwaukee

Visual Communications

Visual Design

Industrial Design

Architecture

Aicher, Otl. *Typographie*. Wilhelm Ernst & Sohn Verlag, Edition Druckhaus Maack, Lüdenscheid, Germany. 1988.

Annenberg, Maurice. *Type Foundries of America and Their Catalogs*. Oak Knoll Press, New Castle, Delaware. 1994.

Anscombe, Isabelle, and Charlotte Gere. *Arts & Crafts in Britain and America*. Academy Editions, London. 1978.

Broos, Kees. *Piet Zwart 1885–1977*. Haags Gemeentemuseum / Van Gennep, Amsterdam. 1982.

Brown, Frank Chouteau. *Letters & Lettering: A Treatise with 200 Examples*. Bates & Guild Company, Boston. 1914.

Dair, Carl. *Design With Type*. University of Toronto Press, Toronto. 1967.

Eason, Ron, and Sarah Rookledge. *Rookledge's International Directory of Type Designers*. The Sarabande Press, New York. 1994.

Elliot, David, ed. *Alexander Rodchenko*. Museum of Modern Art, Oxford. 1979.

Ettenberg, Eugene M. *Type for Books and Advertising*. D. Van Nostrand, Inc., New York. 1947.

Fields, Armond. *George Auriol*. Gibbs M. Smith Inc., Layton, Utah. 1965.

Friedl, Friedrich, Nicolaus Ott, and Bernard Stein, eds. *Typo: Wann, Wer, Wie*. Könemann Verlagsgesellechaft, Köln. 1998.

Gray, Nicolette. *Nineteenth Century Ornamented Types and Title Pages*. Faber and Faber, London. 1938.

Heller, Maxwell L. *New Standard Lettering and Show Card Writer*. Laird & Lee, Chicago. 1926.

Heller, Steven, and Gail Anderson. *American Typeplay*. PBC International, Glen Cove, New York. 1994.

Heller, Steven, and Seymour Chwast. *Graphic Style: From Victorian to Post-Modern*. Harry N. Abrams, New York. 1988.

Heller, Steven, and Anne Fink. *Faces on the Edge: Type in the Digital Age*. Van Nostrand Reinhold, New York. 1997.

Heller, Steven, and Karen Pomeroy. *Design Literacy: Understanding Graphic Design*. Allworth Press, New York. 1997.

Hlasta, Stanley C. *Printing Types and How to Use Them*. Carnegie Press, Pittsburgh. 1950.

Hoffman, Herbert. *Modern Lettering: Design and Application*. William Helburn Inc., New York. Date unknown.

Hollister, Paul. *American Alphabets*. Harper & Brothers Publishers, New York. 1930.

Holme, C. G., ed. *Lettering of To-Day*. The Studio Limited, London. Date unknown.

Hutchings, R. S., ed. *Alphabet 1964*. James Moran Limited, London. 1964.

Jaspert, Pincus W., W. Turner Berry, and A. F. Johnson, eds. *The Encyclopedia of Type Faces*. Blandford Press, Dorset. 1983.

King, Julia. *The Flowering of Art Nouveau Graphics*. Gibbs-Smith Publisher, Salt Lake City. 1990.

Kostelanetz, Richard, ed. *Moholy-Nagy*. Documentary Monographs in Modern Art/Praeger Publishers, New York. 1970.

Lewis, John. *Anatomy of Printing: The Influences of Art and History on its Design*. Watson-Guptil Publications, New York. 1970.

Lewis, John. *Typography: Basic Principles*. Reinhold Publishing Corpoation, New York. 1964.

Lewis, John, and John Brinkley. *Graphic Design*. Routledge & Kegan Paul, London. 1954.

Lindinger, Herbert. *Hochschule für Gestaltung Ulm*. Wilhelm Ernst & Sohn Verlag, Berlin, Germany. 1987.

Massin. *L'ABC du Métier*. Imprimerie Nationale Éditions, Paris. 1988.

McGrew, Mac. *American Metal Typefaces of the Twentieth Century* (Preliminary Edition). The Myriade Press, Inc., New Rochelle, New York. 1986.

McLean, Ruari. *Modern Book Design*. Essential Books, Fair Lawn, New Jersey. 1959.

McMurtrie, Douglas C. *American Type Design in the Twentieth Century*. Robert O. Ballou, Chicago. 1924.

Meggs, Philip, and Rob Carter. *Typographic Specimens: The Great Typefaces*. Van Nostrand Reinhold, New York. 1993.

Nash, Ray. *Printing as an Art*. The Harvard University Press, Cambridge. 1955.

Needham, Maurice H., ed. *The Book of Oz Cooper*. Society of Typographic Arts, Chicago. 1949.

Neuman, Eckhard. *Functional Graphic Design in the 20's*. Rhinehold Publishing Corporation, New York. 1967.

Overy, Paul. *De Stijl*. StudioVista/Dutton, London. 1969.

Pankow, David, ed. *American Proprietary Typefaces*. American Printing History Association. 1998.

Poynor, Rick, and Edward Booth-Clibborn. *Typography Now: The Next Wave*. Booth-Clibborn Editions, London. 1991.

Prokopoff, Stephen S., ed. *The Modern Dutch Poster: The First Fifty Years*. The M.I.T. Press, Cambridge, Massachusetts. 1987.

Reiner, Imre. *Modern and Historical Typography*. Paul A. Struck, New York. 1946.

Richter, Hans. *dada: art and anti-art*. Thames and Hudson, London. 1997.

Rickards, Maurice. *The Public Notice: An Illustrated History*. Clarkson N. Potter, Inc., New York. 1973.

Rogers, Bruce. *Paragraphs on Printing*. William E. Rudge's Sons, New York. 1943.

Ruben, Paul, ed. *Die Reklame: Ihre Kunst und Wissenschaft*. Hermann Paetel Verlag, Berlin. 1914.

Sherbow, Benjamin. *Effective Type-use for Advertising*. Benjamin Sherbow, New York. 1922.

Simon, Oliver. *Introduction to Typography*. Faber and Faber, London. 1963.

Spencer, Herbert. *Pioneers of Modern Typography*. Hastings House, New York. 1969.

Svenson, Carl Lars. *The Art of Lettering*. D. Van Nostrand Company, New York. 1924.

Tschichold, Jan. *The New Typography* (Reprint). University of California Press, Berkeley and Los Angeles. 1995.

Thompson, Susan Otis. *American Book Design and William Morris*. R.R. Bowker Company, New York & London. 1977.

Tracy, Walter. *The Typographic Scene*. Gordon Fraser, London. 1988.

Typomundus 20. Rhinehold Publishing Corporation, New York. 1966.

Warde, Beatrice. *The Crystal Goblet*. World Publishing Company, Cleveland and New York. 1956.